The Mercantile Marine

H.E. INDIA COMPANY'S SHIP *WILLIAM FAIRLIE*

The Mercantile Marine

The story of the merchants
of the seas and oceans

E. Keble Chatterton

LEONAUR

The Mercantile Marine
The story of the merchants
of the seas and oceans
by E. Keble Chatterton

First published under the title
The Mercantile Marine

Leonaur is an imprint
of Oakpast Ltd

ISBN: 978-0-85706-082-2(hardcover)
ISBN: 978-0-85706-081-5 (softcover)

http://www.leonaur.com

Publisher's Notes

In the interests of authenticity, the spellings, grammar and place names
used have been retained from the original editions.

The opinions of the authors represent a view of events in which he
was a participant related from his own perspective,
as such the text is relevant as an historical document.

The views expressed in this book are not necessarily
those of the publisher.

Contents

Preface

This volume is an attempt to trace the history of the Mercantile Marine, and to show the reader how much we owe to our ancestors for the ingenuity, enterprise, courage and perseverance by which the Merchant Service has been built up for the good of nations, the increase of trade and the spread of civilisation. In other volumes I have endeavoured to trace the history of ships. The subject here considered is the birth and growth of a sea service, without which the navies of the world become useless and indeed could never have been brought into being. It is high time that the public appreciated all that is meant by the term Mercantile Marine. The part played by commercial ships as fighting craft during the recent war does not enter into this book. This section was largely treated of in my *Q-Ships and their Story,* and other writers have drawn attention to the dangers and difficulties of freighters and passenger ships carrying on through the period of hostilities. Those four years form so small a chapter in the thousands of years during which the trader has been winning its way across the seas, that it is unnecessary to deal with them here. Our aim is rather to consider the progress of the Mercantile Marine as a whole, from the earliest times to the latest liner development. The story here submitted is the result of many years of research, travel and ship study. I have had access to many manuscripts and printed books too numerous to mention. I desire to return thanks to Messrs. T. H. Parker, 12a Berkeley Street, W., for permission to use some invaluable, rare prints; and to the Cunard and White Star Lines for certain other illustrations of a magnificent service.

E. Keble Chatterton.

CHAPTER 1

Introduction

It is curious to observe how thoroughly most of us are the slaves of habit, how limited we are in our imagination and sympathies until something surprising, far-reaching and inevitable upsets our routine, introduces a new force into our life and compels us to take note of fresh interests.

Until the recent war most people took the Mercantile Marine for granted. In a vague sort of way the average person believed in it, but rarely if ever stopped to consider what it meant or whether it had any history. It was sufficient to concede the fact that there were steamers running every week to most parts of the globe, and that passengers and goods could be carried as convenient.

But there was not the same enthusiasm extended to the Mercantile Marine as there was to the doings of the Royal Navies; and unless some new mammoth steamship advertised herself by her size, speed or luxury, the Merchant Service was allowed to continue its all-important work unheeded and almost despised. But then came the sudden change, which gave an entirely different viewpoint. How few of us ever realise our good fortune until it is taken away from our hold! The increasing success of the U-boat campaign, culminating in the enormous sinkings of merchantmen in April 1917, and the consequent shortage of food in the British Isles, caused the inhabitants for the first time in their lives to appreciate all that they owed to the Mercantile Marine. It was then—and not till then—they reminded themselves that the food supplies, which formed the necessities of life, were brought into the country by a service whose very existence had almost been ignored.

Every meal and every food-card, every little inconvenience in regard to hunger, henceforth turned people's minds back to the prime cause; and those who had been the most ignorant of seafaring matters now began to think in terms of tonnage. From that time the average man and woman and schoolchild have never ceased to be thankful that we had a marine, whose duty was not to fight, but to keep us supplied with the essentials of existence. Admiral of the Fleet Earl Beatty recently said that the Mercantile Marine was a branch of that great sea service without which the British Empire would cease to exist. In a normal year, he said, the amount of food supplies forming the necessities of life which are brought into the British Isles and taken out consists of 150,000,000 tons. Without the one service to carry these food supplies, and the Royal Navy to protect the commercial craft on their lawful occasions, the reader can now well imagine how long starvation would be kept away.

Thus we are about to trace the story of a service that is not merely well deserving of our interest and enthusiasm, but is in itself so fascinating that we shall feel almost ashamed that we never conceded so much attention until harsh circumstances compelled us to reflect. In order to maintain our bread and meat supplies, in order to prevent overseas trade from utterly vanishing during those terrible years of hostilities, 15,000 men of the Mercantile Marine perished. That in itself would be a sufficient reason for inquiring into the history of their service; but, quite apart from that, there is the plea that the Mercantile Marine is the older of the two branches of the sea service, for out of it grew the fighting service only years after man had learnt to handle vessels.

Over those far-distant periods when the ancient seaman was groping his way towards knowledge we shall not require to spend much time. In other volumes I have already traced the evolution of the ship from a crude creature to a thing of beauty. Nor shall we need to be concerned with the horrors of war. Our task is the pleasant and glorious study of watching brave men creating a peaceable marine that will be the means of interchanging commerce overseas at first uncharted; bringing back new ideas and then taking out civilisation. All the time it is one big struggle, varying only in kind and intensity. It is one long, strenuous effort to achieve; and because it is all so human it demands our attention all the while, as we sympathise with the incessant attempts to overcome all sorts of obstacles.

The human race springs from the land: consequently all the arts of the sea have to be learnt from the beginning, and this means centuries of experience, many disappointments and enormous faith and courage. But human aspirations cannot be gainsaid. Progress will not be denied. Man is not content to remain where he was, and that is the basis of the whole story. The Egyptians created their Mercantile Marine almost exclusively for the Nile. It was the Phoenicians who felt the overwhelming desire to traverse the Mediterranean, and even to go outside the gates we call the Straits of Gibraltar. The Greeks inherited from the Phoenicians a ship which they modified but little, as the Phoenicians had from the Egyptians.

But whereas the Egyptians were a peace-loving race, and therefore their ships were not built for fighting, we find the Greeks constructing two distinct types of craft, and it is important to get this quite clear at once, as the reader will presently agree. First there was the swift-moving galley, relying chiefly on oars. She was built for the purposes of fighting, and therefore does not enter into our subject. But secondly there was the slow-moving, big-bellied craft, relying almost entirely on her one mast and sail, which was used for the purpose of trade from spring to autumn, and then laid up until the good weather returned once more. Think of her with her great square-sail going across to Egypt to bring back corn, calling at Rhodes on the way, getting caught in terrible weather, but year after year, century after century, doing the same voyages as a new generation of seamen grew up.

So it was with the Roman merchant ships from every March to November, blundering on their trans-Mediterranean voyages as corn-carriers. These seamen were, as always sailors have been and will be, a race apart. In the mind of most people nobody but a fool or a mad man ever takes up a seafaring career. Seamen were very scarce and had to be allowed special privileges; and merchants who travelled in their ships marvelled that they could use the stars for finding their way over the dark waters at night. But the transportation of goods over the sea had to be done. The ship-owners formed themselves into corporations, and membership was handed down from father to son, much as it is in a fishing village today.

One of the oldest professions is that of piracy. In those days a pirate was not so much a sea bandit as a sea adventurer; the Greek word *peirates* and its Latin equivalent signifying one who attempts or tries his fortune on the sea, much as we speak of the Elizabethan "venturers." None the less, until the growth of naval power piracy always was the great enemy of the merchant ship; and even in Roman times it at length became so serious that drastic measures had to be taken to stamp it out, only to keep on recurring like a cancerous growth until the age of steam practically wiped it out except in Chinese waters. Over and over again in the following chapters we shall see the innocent, cargo-carrying ship molested in this manner; but, for all that, the seaman's spirit remained undaunted, and the trade of the world continued to be carried over the seas in spite of these known risks. As it was in the Mediterranean, so it was later on in the North Sea.

From about 580 B.C. right down to the time of the Roman conquest, the Liparian Isles were practically a republic of *corsairs*. The Ionians and the Lycians were notorious pirates: the Ægean, the Pontus and the Adriatic were the *corsairs'* cruising grounds. The Cretans, the inhabitants of the Balearic Islands, the Cilicians, the Carthaginians, the Illyrians and others, also, were the piratical terrors to the Mediterranean merchant ships; and it was only as long as Rome maintained a strong navy that the cancerous growth was kept under, though not finally eradicated. Thus, in those early periods when there was little enough to encourage it, the Mercantile Marine of classical times struggled along, comparatively small in numbers compared with the fleets of fighting galleys, but historically of the highest importance, since from this small flame was to burst a great blaze of light that has illumined the world; spread Christianity and civilisation, learning, exploration, trade and peace.

Those little, beamy, single-sail, unhandy craft wallowing in the Mediterranean seas, suffering so much at the hands of pirates, buffeted about by storms and compelled to spend such long periods away from their home ports, were playing a lonely, uphill game; but they were achieving more than they could ever realise in the development of the world. Pioneers of the sea, undertaking the utmost risks, they have made all subsequent centuries their debtors as long as ships continue to be built and the seas shall be traversed. Such, briefly, are the first stage and the very remote period of the merchant ship in its long and glorious evolution of usefulness. Let us now see how, influenced by progressive trade, the Mediterranean continued to develop its shipping.

CHAPTER 2

The Demand For Merchant Shipping

In our own age so many amazing developments have taken place during the nineteenth and twentieth centuries that we must not be misled. These are the exceptions and not the rule in history. Between the merchant ships of the late Roman Empire and of the next few centuries there is no evidence to cause us to think the ships materially altered. On the contrary, what little evidence we have goes to show that the cargo ship, with her mast, yard and square-sail, continued to be much the same in the thirteenth century as she was in the third, if we add a mizzen-mast and a lateen sail.

But all this time the Mediterranean trade had been developing, and collaterally there was developed a Mercantile Marine. As the years sped by, there came greater demands for the merchant ship. Thus in the epistles of Cassiodorus, who was *prætorian* prefect under Theodoric (a.d. 495-526), there is a dispatch to the tribunes of the "*maritimi*," or men of the sea-board, bidding them provide for the transport of wine from Istria to Ravenna; and there is a reference to the frequent voyages over the "immense spaces of the sea."[1]

By the eighth century Venice was becoming a great trading port, and its merchants were realising what the sea meant to them in regard to wealth. Indeed, they even went so far as to sell Christian men as slaves to the Saracens in Africa, thus incurring the Pope's censure.

To Constantinople Venetian merchant ships sailed with goods or passengers, as, for instance, in the year 968, carrying Bishop Luitprand

---

1. The Early History of Venice, by F. C. Hodgson. London, 1901. I wish also to acknowledge indebtedness to the same author's Venice in the Thirteenth and Fourteenth Centuries

thither. In fact, by the year 1000 the city of Venice was pre-eminent in commerce, and its princes were merchants. Overseas trading was at last recognised as a means to wealth, and so, inevitably, by about 1171 the Venetian Navy becomes organised. That was bound to come as soon as the Mercantile Marine became important; but it was arranged rather on the lines of our Naval Reserve. For all ordinary occasions it consisted of volunteers, for whose service there was payment, and these citizens were also entitled to prize money.

Indeed, throughout nautical history the navies of the world have always been based on the Merchant Service. In these early days of Venice, while Dalmatia, Istria and other communities supplied the men, Venice provided the ships and rigging, the rest of the inventory and the crew being forthcoming from the dependencies. Finally, in the time of emergency hired seamen were obtained from foreign countries with whom the Venetian commercial ships had traded.

He who visits Venice, or is familiar with Ruskin's *Stones of Venice*, or at least has admired in some gallery the paintings of the great Venetian masters, must inevitably think of the sea. Those richly designed palaces, those luxuriant examples of architecture and art, were expressive of a city grown wealthy by reason of her sea trade. Her merchants amassed wealth because their ships enabled them to trade—the sea is, in fact, the greatest road to riches. And the history of Phoenicia, Egypt, Greece, Rome, Venice, Portugal, Spain, Holland, England in the past, and quite recently Germany, Japan and the United States, is the story of overseas trade by means of merchant shipping. Most important of all have always been the sea routes to the Orient, for Eastern produce has ever fetched high prices in European countries. As we look through the centuries of sea trade it was the fascination of the East which spurred men to build, fit out and sail ships. It was this which gave the incentive to make navigation a science; it was this which created the spirit to explore unknown seas; it was this which sent Columbus, later on, to the West in the hope of finding the East Indies. The whole story of the East India Company—indeed of our Indian Empire—is built up on the invaluable products which could be fetched thence by peaceable shipping.

It was in the seventh century that the twelve townships decided to elect one supreme magistrate, called the "*doge*." Venice thus insisted on her own independence, and her geographical position enabled her to rise into a consummate commercial state. Not merely did she eventually dominate the Adriatic, but step by step she absorbed all the carrying trade of the world. Keen, enterprising men of vision and foresight, these Venetian merchants went far afield, in spite of the difficulties and dangers of travel. For centuries the Chinese had been sending merchant ships as far west as Ceylon, whence Indian ships carried the silk and other goods a stage further west to the Persian Gulf; and afterwards, as there was no Suez Canal, a land journey intervened until the Mediterranean was reached. Thus, by the early years of the Middle Ages, the Venetian ships of commerce brought across the Mediterranean and up the Adriatic the costly skins, the peacocks' tails, the purple garments and other enviable articles which had come from India, the Caspian shores and elsewhere. In the end, Venice captured the great trade to India and China, and Constantinople was left behind in the competition.

But that was not all. Already by the seventh century the rise of Moslem power had become such that in southern Europe Arab dominion had obtained control of the Levant and Egypt. Presently the whole of the north African coast, from the Nile to the Atlantic, fell under this sway, and during the eighth century the Arabs overran Spain, southern and central France, until in the same century they were forced back across the Pyrenees.

How does this affect the rise of the Mercantile Marine? The answer is this. The Arabs were excellent sailors who were also expert navigators, and incidentally the very word "admiral," which still survives in the sea service of all civilised powers, is an Arabic word. The Arabs took to trading, and that meant the employment of ships in the Mediterranean; so they introduced the triangular lateen sail from east of Suez, and to this day the lateen has survived as the characteristic local sail of Mediterranean craft. Thus between Venice and Africa overseas trade was created, business made still further business, and that in turn created a demand for shipping and for men who would use the sea as a career. Later on it was the Arabs who were to teach the Spaniards and Portuguese so much about navigation that India and America were discovered.

In the early years of the Middle Ages, then, we have the Arabian and the Venetian ships trading about the Mediterranean, though frequently the former became *corsairs* and made havoc of the latter, even going to the length of raiding the Adriatic. But so far the peaceable Venetian craft were literally merchant ships: they existed for the purpose of carrying merchandise. There enters now another element-religion. The Catholic faith, trade, pilgrims, crusades and Arabs—all

15

these influences had the greatest possible effect on the development of merchant shipping. It will be remembered that in the seventh century the Arabs had wrested the Holy Land from the Eastern Empire, but it was not until the latter part of the eleventh century that western Europe was really moved to action. Finally, in 1095, a holy war against the infidel was resolved, and there followed the first crusade; and in this expedition Venetian ships took part. The most famous crusade of all was that in which the English king Richard Coeur de Lion engaged, and this ended in a truce with Saladin by September 1192, on the understanding that pilgrims should be permitted to visit Jerusalem without being interfered with by the Moslems.

Thus, we have in the fact of the Holy Land a magnetic attraction for the ship. In order to carry armies and horses and pilgrims, whether from England or Venice, to the coast of Syria, you must needs have large numbers of ships, and of fair size and seaworthiness. This series of voyages created also a much larger body of seamen and amassed a tremendous amount of sea-knowledge from experience. In a word, then, it was a new and enormous impetus to the development of the world's Mercantile Marine, as opposed to the purely war-like fast-moving naval galley. The demand now was for tonnage—to carry human beings as well as goods. Thus, notwithstanding that the crusades originated from a strictly religious motive, actually they exercised a most remarkable stimulus on trade, shipping and travel. Men who had never been previously outside their own city or village became acquainted with the sea, strange ships, new lands and novel ideas. They returned home with fresh aspirations, the desire to carry on extended commerce, and the realisation that shipping was the key to future riches.

To trace the fitting out of all the crusades would be to go outside the scope of our immediate subject, but it is enough if we look for a moment at the direct effect crusading had on the Venetian shipping industry. The gates, so to speak, whence middle Europe could gain access to the Holy Land were Venice, Genoa and Marseilles. Seven years after Richard Coeur de Lion had made the truce with Saladin and left Palestine, a new crusade was being prepared for; and inasmuch as Venice was so distinguished a seaport, envoys came to arrange for large quantities of shipping. Landsmen knew practically nothing about the sea and ships. They were no better informed than the farmer of today resident all his life in the middle of the United States; so they arrived asking for advice, information and generally to be put in the way of obtaining tonnage sufficient to carry 4500 knights, 9000 squires and

20,000 men-at-arms. This was no small order, even for Venice, quite apart from the further request for fifty armed galleys to accompany and protect the expedition. It meant, in fact, the creation of an immense Mercantile Marine at really quite short notice. Indeed it was comparatively a much bigger task than the sudden demand for tonnage in 1917 and 1918, when the thousands and thousands of soldiers had to be packed into steamships and brought from North America to Europe.

Venice rose to the occasion, for it was not merely a matter of business to provide the shipping, but a matter of religion. The Holy Sepulchre was in the hands of the infidels: that in itself was a sufficient inspiration. And so about Pentecost in the year 1202 we can see the hordes of pilgrims pouring down through the various passes of the Alps to Venice. It was a huge business, and action in those days was slow and, to our modern minds, dilatory. But the Venetians had got the ships ready for the knights and squires and men and horses, though it was autumn before they put to sea. Some of the cloth and provisions had arrived in Venice in French ships *via* the Straits of Gibraltar, and eventually, on October 9, the galleys and horse-boats set forth from the Adriatic port, and a month later appeared before Zara.

During the Middle Ages the three great maritime powers were Venice, Genoa and Pisa, and between them there was the greatest rivalry, so that scarcely ever did two of the parties meet than there was conflict. But Venice, being the pre-eminent, incurred the greatest amount of jealousy. The part which Venice and Genoa played in maritime history is not confined to what they did in any particular century, but lies rather in the fact that they kept alive and developed the seaman's art; until, at the beginning of the fourteenth century, the Venetians made a crude map which put into form the ideas that inspired the first Italian voyages in the Atlantic, and Genoa in the next century produced Columbus, who, after being wrecked in a sea-fight with some Venetian galleys off the Portuguese coast, settled down in Lisbon and eventually set forth on his historic voyage to the West.

Ever since the second Punic War Genoa had been a big and important seaport. Becoming a free city in 958, she had suffered much from the Saracen raids, but when these infidel *corsairs* seemed likely to establish themselves in Sardinia at the beginning of the eleventh century, the Genoese and Pisan seamen united together against a common foe, fitted out an expedition and hurled the Arab chief back to Africa. In 1087 the Genoese and Pisans were sent by the Pope to dislodge one Temim, a pirate chief who lived south of Tunis. The result was important to the shipping industry; for, having beaten him and captured his strong-hold, the two cities stipulated for the free admission of their merchant ships to trade with the Tunisian coast. Thus, in clearing the seas of *corsairs* for a time, they also directly stimulated their own commerce.

Pisan merchant ships as far back as 1052 had been trading to Egypt and the Levant, and in 1063 Ingulf, Abbot of Croyland in England, had returned from a pilgrimage in a Genoese merchant ship he had found at Jaffa. But it was not until the year 1090 that the conquest of Sicily was effected from the Mussulman hands, and thus the Straits of Messina became safe for shipping, and the vessels from Genoa and Pisa could go ahead in safety with their Levantine trade. By the twelfth century, Genoese, Venetian and Pisan seamen and merchants used to meet at Acre, to their great financial benefit, though not without manifestations of commercial jealousy. But we must dismiss from our minds all thoughts of single ships sailing across from Italy to the Syrian coast when they liked. There was hardly a time when there were not some pirates or *corsairs* hovering about; so the seas might be rid of one chief, but rendered dangerous by the rovings of another. Thus it was that ship-owners had to do exactly what British mercantile owners were compelled to resort to in the latter part of the Great War, when the enemy was attacking so many of our trading craft—the convoy system had to be employed.

Thus, from Venice, for instance, at regular intervals a convoy of merchant ships would sail for Acre, escorted by as many as thirty or forty galleys sometimes, as protection against piratical attack. If the Venice-Acre trade route were cut, it would mean that the French, the Germans, the Lombards, the Tuscans and other merchants would not receive the silks, sugar, pepper and other very valuable Oriental produce which the Venetians were bringing across in their ships. Thus the navy of Venice was charged with the duty of protecting its merchant fleet from the attacks of Genoese, Greek or Arab pirates. Just as during our recent war convoys used to collect at Falmouth and other ports prior to beginning their ocean voyage, so in the Middle Ages the convoy—called a *mudia*—would collect at Venice, bound for Syria or Egypt. There were only two convoys in the year, so the number of ships was large, and well needed the strong galley protection. One convoy left Venice in the spring and got back home in September; the other left in August, spent the winter abroad, and returned in the following May. In addition to these commercial convoys, there were also the pilgrim convoys to Palestine. Genoa sent one convoy a year to Syria and Egypt, but during the fourteenth century her ships were cruising in the Black Sea and harassing Venetian craft which had penetrated the Sea of Azov.

Sea-travel in those mediaeval times was thus no pleasure cruise: it was comparable only to the anxious experiences of passengers at the height of the recent submarine campaign. Except for religion or trade, no one ever thought of going to sea. It was too dangerous an undertaking, so punctuated with storms, and in all respects so thoroughly uncomfortable, that it was to be avoided as far as possible. Consequently those who used it as a living expected to be paid very handsomely. It is difficult in these modern times, with all the safety and luxury which a steamship connotes, to realise the horror with which all seafaring was regarded.

The result was that artists hesitated to depict marine subjects; and even when they did, it was usually to show a ship having a dreadful time in heavy weather. It is for that reason that illustrations of mediaeval ships are so few, either in stained-glass windows, carvings, devotional books, or paintings. People had no wish to be reminded of what was to them a very unpleasant subject, except to those hardened few who preferred ship-life to agriculture or trade ashore. Unlike present-day conditions, the merchant himself was compelled to go to sea. There was no other means of his reaching his markets; but he was heartily thankful to get himself and his goods safe into port.

CHAPTER 3

The Mediterranean
Mercantile Marine

It is fortunately possible to obtain from various sources an insight into life as it was endured in a mediaeval Mediterranean merchant ship, and this will assist us considerably to form a sympathetic interest in the development which was going on towards the ideal craft that was to evolve five or six hundred years later. On a tomb in a church at Milan, a Pisan artist named Balduccio in the year 1339 sculptured, fortunately for our knowledge, a merchant ship of his time, and we may regard her as typical alike of Venice, Genoa and Pisa. There is remarkably little difference in essentials between her and a Roman merchant ship of about a.d. 200: that is to say, the trading shipmen, having once found out a suitable type, stuck to it, just as today there is a more or less standard type of tramp steamer or steam trawler or steam drifter.

Time had tested and given its approval. Thus in Balduccio's illustration we have a round, beamy vessel not unlike the shape of a very fat banana, and with a stern sweeping up from the water-line not altogether unlike that of the so-called modern "cruiser stern." The essential difference is that this stern culminates in two small decks—a stern-castle, in fact, and a forecastle, much smaller, overhanging the bows. There is also a fighting-top. Although this is emphatically a cargo vessel, these castles and fighting-top are there for the reasons already indicated by existing conditions at sea, and in this elaborate castellation with even small galleries aft we have the half-way house between the earlier and later Mediterranean merchantman: between the cargo-carrier of Rome and the *carack*, which was to develop into the galleon, thence into the East Indiaman, and eventually into the glorious clippers of the late nineteenth century.

Thus this Pisan ship is for us most interesting, and she still links herself to primitive times by the use of one single square-sail and the old-fashioned method of steering by means of a rudder, not aft, but on the quarter. It is controlled by a tiller, but supported by tackles fore and aft, for it is now as heavy as a Thames sailing barge's leeboards.

Everything about this Pisan craft indicates that she was well and strongly built, and that expense was not spared. The elaborate work in her stern galleries, the influence of contemporary land architecture on her forecastle, the stout, thick rubbing strakes under which the ends of the beam come flush, the good strong rigging (three shrouds each side with tackles), the thick cable and the anchor secured to a shelf outside the hull on the starboard side—all these details show that the sculptor knew what he was depicting, and that the ship which he copied was a real sea-going vessel as used by genuine sailormen, and not the inaccurate muddled idea of an imaginative artist. The Pisans, the Venetians and Genoese were making plenty of money, and they could afford to send to sea a well-built, well-designed and well-found craft that would not cause the merchants to feel nervous about their valuable Eastern goods in the hold.

With a mental picture before us of this slow, beamy, stout ship, built specially for seaworthiness and capacity to carry goods, rather than to excel in mobility, we can continue our study, and we shall be able to learn a great deal of the conditions prevailing in the mediæval Merchant Service if we examine the legal literature of the time. For obvious reasons, when there was so much coming and going and so much money at stake, maritime law began to assert itself from about the seventh century *a.d.* onwards, until, about six centuries later, we have practically every contingency catered for.

Between the eighth and the thirteenth centuries there was very little alteration in the ships, the navigation and the manner of sea-trading. The big change comes in the thirteenth century, when the commercial renaissance begins, which, thanks to these vessels, made the great literary and artistic renaissance possible, gave to the world the new learning, the golden age of art, and left behind those wonderful achievements in stone. The merchant ship, therefore, is the basis of all in life that we respect and venerate.

By 1255 Venice had its maritime law, though it was the old so-called Rhodian sea-law,[1] which inspired the regulating of the mediae-

---

1 See *The Rhodian Sea-Law*, edited from MSS. by Walter Ashburner. Oxford 1909. A scholarly and interesting volume.

val merchant ships all the time. The size of a ship was reckoned not in tons, but in *amphorœ* or else in *modii*. An *amphora* represented about six gallons, a *modios* was the equivalent of about two gallons. Thus a ship with all her tackle was valued at fifty pieces of gold for every thousand *modii* of her capacity, though this was further varied according to her age. Port dues at Ancona, for instance, were calculated on the valuation of the ship.

Now it is necessary once more to think of the conditions of service afloat in those days as something quite different from those in our modern Mercantile Marines, where, in spite of trades unions, the captain is supreme and the crew simply carry out his orders, and the passengers have to go wherever he takes them. In those days there was, comparatively speaking, little knowledge of the sea except what was obtained by personal experience. Thus a much-travelled merchant who went backwards and forwards each year to the East would be almost as competent as the master of the ship. Similarly the crew. The result was—and it seems very strange to us moderns—that the ship was run not on a well-disciplined principle, as everyone obeying blindly the master's orders, but on a communal basis, backed up by the maritime law. Sometimes, it is true, the sailors were paid fixed wages, in which case they were also given their food; but frequently they undertook the voyage on a profit-sharing basis. Thus the master received two shares, the steersman one and a half, the master's mate one and a half, the boatswain one and a half, while each sailor got a whole share, and the cook half a share. It was therefore to the interest of all to do everything to get the ship safely from port to port.

The little difference which existed between master, officers, men and merchants enabled them all in an emergency to offer their opinions as to weather, pilotage and so on, a decision being arrived at by the vote of the majority. All this sounds thoroughly unseamanlike to us, but that is because the seafaring art has long since become so perfect and systematised, and the division of labour recognised as a root essential. It was perfectly legal for the merchants, with their valuable goods on board, to insist on the ship being taken into a harbour, or to prevent her putting to sea notwithstanding all the protests of the *naukleros* or shipmaster. The identity of ignorance among all on board, with the casting vote in favour of finance, bred chaos and ill-discipline, that had to be put down with a firm hand later on, as soon there arose competent navigators and specialists in seamanship; but the time had not yet come.

No one can possibly envy the life in a merchant ship of the Middle Ages, with every possible opportunity for friction and the captain not allowed a free hand. The passenger came on board in fear and trepidation, bringing with him his own bed and bed-coverings, which, as happened in 1278, for instance, were stolen from him occasionally. A proper cabin he could not have, the sleeping space permitted to him being three cubits long and one cubit wide. Under the Venetian statutes every merchant or mariner could take on board free one mattress; the former could also have one trunk, but this was not allowed to his servant. The passengers brought with them for the voyage all their food, wine, cooking utensils, and even their firewood, but there were special precautions taken to guard against fire, which was one of the eternal terrors in all ships even down to the nineteenth century. Thus there is a curious regulation preventing passengers in Venetian ships from frying fish, and another forbidding them to split wood. Water was supplied free both to passengers and crew, but this was controlled by measure, for economical reasons.

Arrived on board, the passenger would deposit his gold with the captain for safe keeping. He lived on biscuits, salt meat, vegetables, cheese, onions, garlic and vinegar, and there was a Barcelona ordinance of 1258 which compelled the ship-owner to keep a supply of food to last fifteen days, and this was to include bread, wine, salt meat, vegetables, oil and water. As regards victualling, cargo ships found it easier than pilgrim ships, for the former could usually hug the shore and put into the land for provisions. Indeed it was one of the characteristics of a good pilot that he knew where the ship could obtain fresh drinking water.

The merchant, with his costly goods, out of which he hoped to make big profits, found himself in the company of rough mariners who were lacking the innocence of the carved saints in a cathedral. Thieving was going on all the time whenever there was a chance. Nowadays you sometimes hear one seaman describe another as so dishonest that he would steal the ship's anchor if he could. It is an obvious exaggeration, but the expression was perfectly accurate in the times of which we are now speaking. There was a passage in the maritime law which dealt with this species of theft. Thus, it runs, if a ship not under way was robbed of her anchors, and the thief was caught and confessed, he was to be flogged and to make good twice the damage. Similarly, if a sailor robbed a merchant or the captain, he was to be punished, and there are penalties laid down against swearing, blasphemy and other vices.

In these wooden ships, which often "worked," and had to go through heavy weather, the merchant would sometimes find his beautiful Oriental silks ruined; so there was a regulation that when the water began to rise in the hold the captain was to let the merchants know at once, so that they could bring their linens and silks up on deck. But apart from these risks there were those caused by bad seamanship, the attacks by pirates at sea or robbers in harbour, the evil men who did not hesitate to cut the cables of the visiting ship or waylay the merchants and crew as soon as they came ashore; and there were the wreckers who deliberately displayed false lights to lure the ship into destruction—surely one of the lowest of all maritime crimes that could be devised by the cunning of man.

It was laid down that if a ship "in sail" ran into another ship lying at anchor, or which had "slackened sail," and it was during daylight, the damage was to be borne by the captain, by those on board and by the cargo. But if the incident occurred at night, the man who "slackened sail" should have lit a fire or have shouted. Be it remembered that these merchant ships, though the most seaworthy of any craft then in existence, were very unhandy and not always under control in narrow channels. It was impossible for any regulation of man to prevent them encountering bad weather and even experiencing shipwreck, but by laying these ships up in November, and not allowing them to sail until the following March, the authorities were following the wise custom which had been handed down since classical times, and embodied this practice in their law. Against the *corsair* who attacked the ships of his country's enemies, and against the pirate who attacked every ship that came his way, there could be no absolute guarantee unless the ship was in a convoy escorted by armed galleys.

But these *corsairs* made no false pretence about their work, and when in 1165 the Pisans asked Trepedecinus, a well-known Genoese *corsair*, where he was going, he merely replied that he was going to capture them, their goods, their persons and cut off their noses. It was therefore not unusual to carry in these trading ships some men-at-arms with swords, shields and helmets. Thus, in a charter-party of 1236 there is laid down that there are to be twenty-five mariners on board, of whom ten are to be in armour. Quite apart from the convoy system, it was customary for two or more ships to voyage in company for mutual protection, the technical term for this being *conservagium*. It was an arrangement that was mutual also in quite another manner, for if one of the ships was sunk, the loss was spread among the others in the consort—a still further instance of the sharing-out principle which was so common at sea in these times.

Gradually, then, the Mercantile Marine had become indispensable to trade and to intellectual progress, but it was the growth of pilgrim traffic which made certain landsmen affluent; for now men called *cargatores*, or passenger agents, arranged the business of transporting these devout people across the sea, and therefore stringent regulations had to be passed to prevent the travellers from being fleeced. Thus the *cargatores* were compelled to supply the pilgrims with good and adequate victuals; and, in order to prevent any bribery or corruption, they were forbidden to enter into partnership with the ship-owner in regard to the food. Of course this was no small undertaking at a period of the world's history when there were no such things as preserved meats or refrigerating chambers, especially when the ships were crowded with a lot of seasick landsmen who had never previously beheld the sea. All those who voyaged from Venice or Marseilles had to carry enough food to last them for fifty days, and in those rough ships and the Mediterranean climate you can imagine the state of the food at the end of seven weeks. No wonder that a pilgrimage was a real act of self-denial!

It was customary in classical times to give names to the Mediterranean ships, and this survived through the Middle Ages, where we find such names as *Urso, Oliva, Aguila, Christiana, Cidona, St. Blazius*. The Genoese ship went by the name of her shipmaster or owner. After she had been built and fitted out, the greatest care was taken to see that she was seaworthy and not overloaded. Thus the internal arrangements, the ballasting and stowing of goods in the hold were all supervised. The Venetian statutes kept a very tight control over their shipping, regulating the places where the cabins were to be put, where the sail locker should be, where the ship's tackle was stored, and the sleeping arrangements both for the merchants and the sailors. No detail seems to have been too small for State supervision.

The stowing of the cargo in the hold was left to the discretion of the shipmaster, and there was a kind of Plimsoll mark used in these Venetian ships; for this is what happened. On the outside of the hull a mark was put, the ship was then loaded and examined officially before setting forth on her voyage, and she was not allowed to proceed to sea if this mark was more than a certain depth below the water-line, this depth varying according to the ship's age. If the mark were submerged too much, a sufficient quantity of cargo had to be taken out until she came up to her marks, and then the owner was fined. This was the general rule, but exceptions were made in the case of craft sailing within the Venetian Gulf or carrying victuals.

The ballasting of the merchant ships was done either by the navigating officer or else under the direction of a committee composed of this officer and representatives of owners and merchants. But when once the vessel had been properly ballasted, it was forbidden to remove any ballast except for necessity in entering port, or with the consent of the merchants or committee, though certain heavy articles, such as lead, were permitted to be substituted for ballast. The heavy goods were, of course, placed as low as possible, though such articles as wrought silks and other light goods were allowed to bestowed on the upper deck, where also food, carpenter's tools and armour could be placed.

The owner of the ship was also at times her master, but when the owner did not himself go to sea and himself appointed the master, he contracted to carry the passengers and cargo, purchased the tackle and engaged the seamen. Right down to Elizabethan times the navigation of the ship was not necessarily carried out by the captain, but by the pilot, though in the early days of Mediterranean merchant shipping the masters seem to have been navigators as well, or, more accurately, pilots. If the ship got wrecked there was, according to an old constitution of a.d. 880, a practice of obtaining the true facts of the incident in a manner far more drastic than a modern Board of Trade Inquiry; for certain members of the crew would be selected as witnesses, and they were then tortured until they should speak the whole truth and nothing but the truth.

The communal idea even went to the length of having sometimes several skippers on the same ship, in order that no one should act without the consent of the others; and what with the interfering advice and remonstrances of the merchants and the not too disciplined crews, no mercantile officer of today would find mediaeval seafaring endurable. The mariners could only be kept in check by the drastic law. Thus, if one of them injured another, the first was to pay his wages to the other during the whole time that the sick man was out of employment recovering. Conversely the captain was prevented from maltreating his men, and had to look after them. For instance, if the ship's long boat with some of the crew in it should break adrift from the ship, the captain had to pay the lost men's representatives their wages for a whole year, in those cases where the men were in receipt of wages instead of a share of the profits.

There were plenty of opportunities for disgruntled mariners to forsake the ship at the ports of call. In order to check this, the man who deserted his ship was liable to forfeit double his wages received or due. The usual custom was to engage the hands from the 1st of March to the last day of November, and they received their pay on the 1st of March, the 1st of June and the 1st of September. This did not mean that the vessel necessarily put to sea at the beginning of March, but in order to be sure of his men the *naukleros* hired them before they were actually required. Having once been engaged, the mariners were forbidden by statute to leave the city, but at Pisa, when the ship was about to sail, a crier was sent round collecting the men.

It was not part of their duty to load or unload the cargo: that was done by the stevedores, but it did fall to them to ballast the ship. Each mariner, on being engaged, took an oath that he would carry out his duties, and he had to obey the master. The only occasions on which he could justifiably quit his ship were if he were made captain of another ship, or if he had made a vow to go on a pilgrimage to St. James or the Holy Sepulchre or Rome. On the other hand, he could be dismissed for theft, quarrelling, repeated disobedience, blasphemy or debauchery. At Pisa, if a mariner made a disturbance on board, the captain and other officials could put him into irons, and if he resisted they could strike him even to the drawing of blood.

No merchant of the twentieth century sending his goods across the seas would have need to inquire into the inventory or seaworthiness of the ship. Such things are taken for granted; but even in the carefully regulated conditions of these old Mediterranean ships, it was customary for merchants before putting their goods aboard to see that the vessel was well furnished with sails, yards, anchors and arms, for she should carry spare yards and sails of canvas (doubtless for hard weather), as well as other gear. The merchants were also to ascertain that the ship was water-tight, and the skipper was to fill up the seams with tow. The Venetian statutes prescribed that a ship should have so many anchors and ropes of a certain length and thickness. And thus, at last, with anything from sixteen to forty mariners—according to her size—with her merchants, their servants, men-at-arms and pilgrims and cooks, the trading vessel was allowed to go forth.

Such, then, were the conditions under which the Mercantile Marine was emerging during these interesting years. Like other nations,

Venice began to lose her commercial supremacy soon after the Cape of Good Hope had been discovered in 1486. The future of the overseas trading was to be in the hands of Portugal and Spain, then to pass into the control of the Dutch, the French, and subsequently into British hands, as some day it may fall under the direction of the United States. But the important fact to remember all the while is that Venice, Genoa and Pisa did demonstrate to the world that civilisation, progress, literature, art, riches, exploration all depended on the merchant ship. Having once proved the truth of this idea, they have left behind for us in their contemporary buildings the most striking expressions of the wealth that is obtained only by means of the sea.

CHAPTER 4

The Merchant Ships of the North

We can desire hardly any better evidence of the existence of a Mercantile Marine than the fact that a body of laws had to be created in order to regulate that industry. We have seen that from quite early times there was in the Mediterranean a sea-law which in course of time was available for any set of circumstances that might arise in regard to trading ships.

In like manner there came into being a code of maritime laws for western Europe, and this was known as the Laws of Oleron. The code was adopted by Alfonso X in the thirteenth century for the settlement of disputes in maritime affairs. It was based on the sea-law of Rhodes already referred to. Now, one effect of the crusade which Richard Coeur de Lion undertook was that he came into contact with a number of ships and seamen who had been sent from the island of Oleron to take part in the crusade. And among the officers who had come with the fleet from Oleron was one of the justiciaries of the navy.

The net result was that Richard brought home a roll of these laws, and ordered them to be observed in English waters. They had been framed for the benefit of the Merchant Service, and they were drastic. Thus if a pilot lost the ship and the merchants sustained damage, the pilot was to make full satisfaction, if he had the means; if he had no means he was to lose his head. Now, based on these laws of Oleron, came into being what was known as the "Black Book of the Admiralty," which contained the "ancient statutes of the Admiralty, to be observed both upon ports and havens, the high seas and beyond the seas, which are engrossed upon vellum in the said book and written in an ancient hand in the ancient French language," as a High Court Judge of the seventeenth century described them.

This so-called "Black Book" contains the most ancient laws of the sea in force in this country, and continued to be the standard authority in the Admiralty Court until the end of the eighteenth century, when it suddenly disappeared, but in 1874 it was accidentally discovered at the bottom of a chest belonging to a former Registrar of the Admiralty Court. Today this book is kept in a glass-topped, locked table in the room of the President of the Admiralty Court. It was probably called black to distinguish it from other books of reference, but the late Sir Douglas Owen, who had examined it about the year 1911, said that the cover was now very much the colour of a worn-out leather strap. It measures 9½ inches high and 6¼ inches wide, the leaves being either thin parchment or a stout tough paper.

The first part of the book is written in archaic French, but it was not all written at one time nor by one person. In other words, as the Merchant Marine of England grew in numbers and importance, as the trade with the continent got bigger, so the English maritime law kept up with the progress. The first part of the "Black Book" belongs to the time of Edward III or Richard II, the latter part to the time between Henry IV and Henry VI. Thus, part of the book shows that the English Mercantile Marine was of sufficient size and importance in the period between 1327 and 1351 to necessitate a body of laws.

In character the ships of Northern waters were based on those of the Norsemen—that is to say, they were double-ended, long, and propelled by one large square sail, or with oars when necessary. As time went on, these craft became beamier, and approximated to the cargo ships of the Mediterranean, the twofold objects aimed at being sea-worthiness and capacity for carrying as much as possible in their holds. But there is this important fact to bear in mind, and its value can hardly be exaggerated, as we shall presently find. The North Sea has from the earliest records until the present day been the home of the herring, and on the herring the nations of the North have prospered, built their Mercantile Marines, grown rich, created their navies and expanded commercially. The fishing fleets have only to put to sea and they can extract silver fortunes—it is, so to speak, money for nothing, or for very little. That is the broad, general statement, though in practice it is modified by the migrations of the herring, which did actually alter the trend of history.

As far back as the third century the inhabitants of the Hebrides were living on fish and milk, but ignorant of the cultivation of grain, and even in the ninth century the Dutch came to Scotland to buy salted fish. In the tenth century the Norwegians were fishing with their herring-nets near Christiania, and off the East Anglian coast our own fishermen were pursuing the industry on a large scale. Before William the Conqueror arrived, Beccles, then a fishing town (but now inland on the banks of a river), paid as rent to St. Edmund's Abbey as much as 30,000 herrings. In France by 1030 the herring-fishing was a well-established occupation, and there were salt works near Dieppe for preserving the catches. During the twelfth century our fishermen found herrings very plentiful off the Tyne. Further north the English, Scotch and Belgic fishermen were getting the herring near May Island off the Firth of Forth, and in this same period the herring was being first fished for in the Meuse. The Dutch were sending out small vessels to use their nets in the North Sea, then later on packing the fish into barrels, preserving them by cleaning their insides and thus beginning to acquire wealth from the harvest of the sea.

Thus the North Sea fisheries were to build up the Mercantile Marines of the North. We were exporting herrings, wool, butter, cheese and cattle to the continent via the Rhine, and already during the thirteenth century a big Lorraine fleet, carrying cargoes of wine, used to arrive annually in England; but it was the impetus given by the herring that caused the north European countries to develop the sea instinct. The fishing industry developed shipbuilding, created a great seaman- hood, spread the fascination of the sea as a career, and thus handed down from century to century a great and wonderful school, from which in Tudor times were to be obtained the crews who ventured forth with Drake and others. You cannot suddenly bring into being this seafaring body, as you can collect armies.

And had it not been that for hundreds of years the Englishmen had been out fishing, there would have been no expansion of England either commercially or politically. The history of the world would, indeed, have to be rewritten. By the time of Edward III the fishing had become so important to this country that a law was passed forbidding any fisherman to give up his trade; but, in return for this, fishermen and mariners were exempt from serving in any capacity other than that to which they had been bred. By the fourteenth century there were literally thousands of vessels, each having at least six persons on board, fishing for herrings between Denmark and Norway, and more than 300,000 people were in one way or another engaged in the industry.

In five days no fewer than sixty foreign ships during one week came into Great Yarmouth for these fish. Thus, side by side with our fishermen there was growing up a carrying trade, herrings and woollen cloth being regularly exported to the continent. By the fifteenth century ships from the British Isles, France, Flanders, Zeeland, Holland and Germany with Scottish herrings used to sail to the Mediterranean to sell the fish for the faithful during Lent.

Throughout the Middle Ages the herring-fishing of the North Sea was far and away the most important of western Europe, especially off Scotland, Sweden and Norfolk, whither the Dutchmen came both to use their nets and to buy. The trade in salted and smoked herrings helped to make the wealth of the Hanseatic and Dutch towns. And it is here that we find, in the Hanseatic League, a force which corresponds to that of Venice, Pisa and Genoa in the south; for in developing overseas trade it encouraged the ship and seafaring. The word "*hansa*" signifies a guild or association, and the Hanseatic League was an association of towns for the purposes of trade, Bergen, London and Bruges being its principal foreign markets in the North Sea. From the twelfth to the sixteenth century this trading league existed, and, like Venice, had its rise to pre-eminence and then gradually lost its supremacy. And, like Venice, too, the Hanseatic League kept a tight hand over its merchant ships.

Thus as far back as 1391 there was an ordinance by the Diet that no merchant should sail from a North Sea to a Baltic port, or vice versa, between Martinmas and Candlemas, and the only exceptions were that ships carrying beer and herrings might sail as late as St. Nicholas Day, December 6. For centuries a merchant had signified a townsman, but when, from the beginning of the twelfth century, the herring suddenly arrived in great shoals in the Baltic, the inland dwellers of Germany came down to the sea, ousted the Slav and thus began to get rich. The movements and migrations of the herring are little more understood nowadays than they were then, but it was sufficient for the Hanseatics that this silvery wealth had arrived. Thus Kolberg became a famous emporium for salted herrings, and this fishing industry was responsible for the Hansa towns obtaining so much of their riches and power. And so it went on until, in 1425, the erratic herring decided to forsake the Baltic and spawn in the waters of the North Sea. This at once took away from the Hanseatics a large portion of their means to wealth, though they were still busy with their carrying trade. But what is one country's loss may be another's gain, and it was so with the herring.

For from the Baltic the herring had moved down to the Dutch

coast, and so the Netherlands found themselves with the good fortune of a silver mine outside their own doors. Riches were there for the asking, and they wisely availed themselves of the opportunity. They built more ships, and the whole waterside went forth in clumsy, seaworthy craft, and thus gradually the fishermen laid the foundation-stone of the Dutch nation.

It is an old saying that *Amsterdam was built upon herrings; and as the Venetian palaces were built on Eastern pepper and silks,* so the Northern capital arose out of the efforts on sea. It is impossible to appreciate all that the herring-fishery has meant to Holland until one has been through all the picture galleries in the Low Countries and explored its harbours. In the former you find the herring busses riding to their nets as the subject of any number of paintings, for the reason that it was the most important aspect of Dutch livelihood; and around the quays today you have only to notice the fine architecture in order to see the relics of a wealth that came and passed away by means of the sea high-road.

There is nothing like trade for the encouragement of shipping, but it was not until the end of the thirteenth century that the inland towns of the continent required for their trade the highway of the ocean, and thus the ports became important and the demand for shipping increased. One of the most important of the Hanseatic sea-trade routes was from Bruges to northern Russia, whither hundreds of craft sailed every year, owned by the Baltic merchants. And it was not until the fifteenth century that the Dutchmen, Zeelanders and Frisians seriously competed with the Hanseatics, for the latter was a very close corporation, whose organisation was kept secret, and its ban was regal in its effect.

By its decree no German merchant was allowed to go into partnership with an Englishman, Fleming or Russian, and the result was that for centuries our shipping was kept out of the Baltic. All this time the Hanseatic trade was doing a great deal to encourage its own shipping, for there were needed many craft and seamen to carry eastwards from Germany to Russia the produce of the looms and the breweries, returning with furs, wax, skins, tallow and fat. Similarly the shipping went across to Sweden to fetch the copper and iron, while to Bruges and London this Russian and Swedish produce was brought for distribution.

As in the cargo ships of the Mediterranean, so here in the north, the merchants accompanied their wares "over sea and sand." Some of them would mutually arrange to charter a ship, and in order to encourage the captain to get the goods safely across the sea, they would give him an interest in the sales. Otherwise, as soon as pirates hove into sight he might feel inclined to hurl the goods overboard, and a similar desire was thus checked in the case of the ship labouring in bad weather.

Piracy in the English Channel, Irish Sea, North Sea and the Baltic went on merrily during the Middle Ages, and played havoc with the merchant ship, though, as in the south, this kind of activity was less a crime than a specialised form of seafaring. In the Cinque Ports dwelt a class of seamen commissioned, according to Matthew of Paris, to plunder all merchant ships of any nationality other than English as they passed up and down the Channel; so in the thirteenth century we find the Scotch, Irish, Welsh and French all fitting out vessels to cruise about in readiness for a cargo ship full of valuable goods.

The English Channel and the North Sea thus became full of dangers, and no merchant ship could put to sea without grave risk of capture. One nationality was as bad as another, and a kind of international vendetta went on in revenge for the losses by piracy. It became, indeed, a matter of high politics, far too serious to be ignored, so that the kings of England at various dates had to enter into negotiations with the foreign authorities. Thus at the beginning of the fifteenth century the Chancellor of England demanded from the Master-General of Prussia full restitution and recompense for "sundry piracies and molestations offered of late upon the sea."

During the next reign Henry IV, writing to the same personage, admitted that both English and Prussian merchants had suffered by these pirates "roving up and downe the sea." It was finally agreed that English merchant ships should be allowed to enter Prussian ports unmolested, and that if Prussian cargoes were captured in the North Sea by English pirates, and this merchandise was brought into an English port, the "governour" of the port, if he suspected piracy, was to have such goods taken out and put ashore in safe keeping. And between this same Henry and the Hanseatic towns a similar agreement was made which bound the cities of Lubeck, Bremen, Hamburg and others to recompense the injured parties "for all injuries, damages, grievances, and drownings or manslaughters" done and committed by the pirates.

The following incidents well illustrate the risks which these merchantmen ran whilst pursuing their calling. About Eastertide in the year 1394 the merchant ship *Godezere*, owned by four Englishmen, set out from the Tyne for Prussia, loaded with a cargo of woollen cloth and red wine. She was a 200-ton ship, her value with that of her sails and tackle amounting to £400; her cargo, plus certain sums of money on board, aggregating 200 *marks*. In the North Sea she encountered a Hanseatic ship who gave the English craft such a hot time that the *Godezere* was captured, two of her crew slain, and the rest of them were imprisoned for three years. In the same year the Hanseatic pirates also attacked the Hull ship named the *Skipper Berline of Prussia*, belonging to a Richard Horuse, and from her they took away goods to the value of 160 nobles.

Next year, off the coast of Norway, they molested a ship called the *John Tutteburie*, and relieved her of 476 nobles worth of cargo. A year later still, these Hanseatic pirates captured the Hull ship *Cogge*, belonging to one William Terry, and took £200 worth of woollen cloth as well. The pirates were no respecters of ships so long as valuable goods were being taken across the North Sea, for Dutch, Zeeland and English merchantmen and fishing craft were all made to suffer. If the merchants and crew were not killed, they were thrown into prison and not allowed their liberty until ransom was paid, so altogether the trading ship had quite as exciting a time in the north as in the southern sea.

But it was just as bad in the Baltic, where the pirates found it such a profitable business that they formed themselves into a corporation, and became such a serious and powerful force that in 1392 they were able to burn down Bergen and take the bishop prisoner. This much is to be said for them: they had a sense of chivalry, and on occasions actually gave back the empty ships to merchants after removing the cargoes, and wished them a happy return with fresh and fuller freights. But so mighty a scourge did these sea-raiders become that for a time they put a stop to all fishing. In the spring of 1394 these lawless Hanseatics sailed with quite a large fleet to the town of Norbern in Norway, took the place by assault, captured all the merchants, together with their goods, burnt their houses and put their persons up to ransom.

Matters had now reached a crisis. For three years all fishing had been stopped and these rovers had made maritime life impossible, so in 1394, by means of a tax, the Hanseatic League got together a fleet of thirty-five large ships and 3000 men, and by this means broke the power of this pirate confederation—for a time; for the scourge continued for years after. It was a fine life for those who had run through their money and desired adventure, and it attracted men of noble birth who had gambled and drunk away their fortunes. Of these none was more notorious than Stertebeker, who took part in almost every instance of North Sea piracy at this time. Hamburg having denied to this reprobate his knightly armour and forbidden him the city precincts, he threw in his lot with the notorious pirates known as the Victual Brothers, whose leader was Godeke Michelson.

There was no limit to the depredations of this band. On one occasion they attacked a ship in the North Sea named the *Dogger*, which was lying at anchor while the crew were fishing. These Hanseatics took away their fish, beat and wounded both master and crew, and owing to the damage done lost the *Dogger* a whole year's fishing. Nor did the daring of the pirates confine itself to the Baltic and North Sea: they even raided the coast of Spain. Stertebeker was one of those heavy-drinking Germans who had a curious method of dealing with his prisoners; for if among them he found a poor, strong man he would test the latter's powers by resort to drinking. Stertebeker, whose own *mark* consisted of two reversed goblets in a cathedral church, would cause his own goblet to be filled with wine and handed to the prisoner. If the latter could empty it at one gulp, he was a man after Stertebeker's heart, and was accepted as a comrade, otherwise he was dismissed.

But there came a time when this terror to the merchant ships of all nations had reached the limit. In the year 1422 the Hanseatic League sent a fleet under Simon of Utrecht to fall upon the pirates, and having come out from Hamburg, Simon found the enemy one evening lying off Heligoland. So near did the Hamburg fleet get to them that one daring fisherman was able to pour molten lead on the rudders of certain of the pirate ships, and this loosened the rudders and rendered the ships uncontrollable.

On the following day the battle began, and went on for three days and nights, but in the end Stertebeker was beaten. He and seventy of his comrades were captured and carried in triumph to Hamburg, where they were all condemned to death and executed, to the great relief of the mercantile mariners. The rest of the pirates had fled, or been killed or thrown into the sea, and in the captured ships were found much linen and wax and cloth, which had been ill gotten from unfortunate craft. But when the Hamburgers rummaged the ships all the valuable metals they could find were a few goblets: until a carpenter broke the mainmast, which was then found to be hollow, and full of molten gold. However, this conveniently indemnified the merchants, and a golden crown was made and placed on the spire of St. Nicholas church, Hamburg. Stertebeker's friend and accomplice, Michelson, was still at large, but Simon went after him, got him, and eighty pirates lost their heads.

CHAPTER 5

The Growth of the Mercantile Merchant

Chaucer, who flourished in the fourteenth century, has left us a description of a merchant "shipman" of his time. He refers to him as being a West-countryman living, "for aught I woot," at Dartmouth, who wore a gown of coarse cloth extending to the knee, and had a dagger hanging on a lanyard. The hot summer had tanned his face brown, and Chaucer describes him as a good fellow, who had drawn many a draught of wine while the "*chapman*" (or merchant) was asleep. No man had such skill in reckoning his tides, streams, dangers; and in his knowledge of harbours, the state of the moon and pilotage, there was no such man between Hull and Carthage.

> Hardy he was, and wys to undertake:
> With many a tempest hadde his herd been shake.
> He knew wel alle the havenes, as they were,
> From Gootlond to the cape of Finistere,
> And every cryke in Britayne and in Spayne:
> His barge y-cleped was the Maudelayne.

From the mere fact that Chaucer said as much as he did, it is clear enough that English merchant ships at this time were trading up and down Europe between Sweden and the Spanish coast, and that as a regular thing. And some of these seamen were now also navigators. Chaucer, who died in the year 1400, has left behind a treatise on the astrolabe by which a mariner could "knowe the altitude of the Sonne, or of other celestial bodies." An astrolabe was the ancestor of the sextant, an instrument which had been used by the Arabs for long years before it was used by the Christian seamen of the Mediterranean or the North. As far back as the eighth century a learned Rabbi named Messahala had written a treatise on the astrolabe, and it was chiefly from that author that Chaucer derived his knowledge on the subject. During the early Tudor period the cross-staff began to supersede the astrolabe.

The growth of the English Mercantile Marine in the fourteenth century, and the friction which occurred between these ships and the vessels belonging to Norway, Prussia, Flanders, Scotland, Spain and Genoa, led to the assertion by Edward III that his royal progenitors had been lords of the English sea "on every side," and in 1344 he had coined a gold *noble* whereon he was represented standing in a ship crowned, with sword and shield, emblematic of his sovereignty of the seas. It was a statesmanlike attempt on behalf of the commercial ships to make the sea a peaceful highway, when for so long it had been such a dangerous thoroughfare. It had its counter-part in the Mediterranean; for the raids by the Saracens had caused the Pisans to exercise the rights of commercial and naval supremacy on the west coast of Italy; and in 1138 the Genoese had exercised a similar authority in the Gulf of Lyons. Similarly Venice had claimed sovereignty over the whole of the Adriatic in the thirteenth century, though prior to that it had exacted a toll from vessels passing through that sea.

England, too, had her pilgrim trade to Santiago de Campostela, thirty-three miles south of Corunna, where the shrine of St. James caused these travellers to cross the Bay of Biscay to Spain. By the fifteenth century this transportation of pilgrims had become a regular trade, and in 1434 Henry VI granted a licence to carry no fewer than 2433 such enthusiasts. Indeed the earliest English sea song is that which describes the life on board one of these pilgrim ships. The manuscript is in the Trinity College Library, Cambridge, and it begins by saying that "men may leve all gamys, that saylen to Seynt Jamys," for when these people have joined the ship at Sandwich, Winchelsea, Bristol or wherever it may be, their hearts soon begin to fail, "for som ar lyke to cowgh and grone, or hit be full mydnyght."

The cook is ordered to get food ready, but the pilgrims have "no lust" for eating, but lie "with they bowlys fast them by" and complaining that their heads would "cleave in three"—"splitting," as the modern martyr to sea-sickness expresses it. Then the carpenter comes along and with his gear makes small cabins for the unhappy passengers to sleep in. A sack of straw formed the mattress, and in some cases the pilgrims found they had to sleep near the pump and bilge-water in the reeking hold. "A man were as good to be dede, as smell thereof the stynk." For there are few odours more objectionable than the bilge-stench of an aged ship, and in those days, when refuse was thrown into the hold and there was little idea of sanitation, a pilgrim's voyage from England to Spain, across the boisterous Bay, could not have been more pleasant than from Venice to the Syrian shore.

In this poem just quoted it is interesting to notice, also, the life on board the merchant ship as regards the mariners. We see the master at once ordering his "shyp-men" to stand by the mast and handle their tackle. Then, with the old expression of the sea (still surviving in sailing merchant vessels today), "Ho! Hissa," they hoist away, whilst one man reprimands another for standing too close to his neighbour to allow him room to haul. Then one or two boys go up aloft, out on the yard, and unfurl the square-sail, while the rest of the crew haul aft the sheets. The captain then orders the boatswain to stow the ship's boat, and next " haul the bowline," the ship being now on a wind; but presently "veers the sheet" to allow her to run before the breeze. The steersman is sent to the helm and told to sail no nearer to the wind, after which the master calls the steward to bring him a pot of beer, which is promised "with good chere." It is now time to haul in the brails of the yard, and one of the crew is admonished for not hauling; and then see "howe well owre good shyp sayles." The steward is told to get food ready "and tary not so long," whilst the ship's pessimist comes and prophesies a storm or squall. He is promptly told to hold his "pese" and not to interfere.

Then commeth oure owner lyke a lorde.
And speketh many a royall worde,
And dresseth hym to the hygh horde
To see all thyng be well.

Thus, with the demand for shipping to carry cargo and pilgrims across the open sea, there was every chance given to the Mercantile Marine, and by the fifteenth century the single-masted ship had begun to be displaced by the three-master, for the reason that the merchantman was becoming bigger, and it was necessary to split the sails up for ease in handling. Thus the big cargo ship now has a small square foresail on her foremast, a big square mainsail on her mainmast, and a triangular lateen sail on the mizzen-mast. The mere fact that the last-mentioned, characteristic, Mediterranean sail was added to northern ships during the fifteenth century, is evidence of the influence which the Portuguese and Spanish ships were having on our distant-voyaging vessels. Sea transportation was becoming the rule, and no longer the exception; trade overseas was increasing; merchants and seamen were fast becoming imbued with new ideas seen in strange lands, and in fact the world was beginning to awake.

The biggest of the ships carried a main topsail, and by this time the rudder had been shifted from the quarter to aft, as it is today. The hull is in a transition state, still feeling the influence of the Viking type, but not yet a wholesome creature. The forecastle, sterncastle and main topmast castle are still there, but they have become amalgamated with the general design of the hull rather than being mere additional platforms. There is a contemporary manuscript which shows such craft under way, at anchor, and even being towed out of harbour by the ship's boat against a head wind, past a flaming beacon which marks a promontory. And even at this time there were such things as pilots' guides for the coasts of England and Wales, as well as sailing directions for the Bay of Biscay.

But we must turn our attention south to watch what was going on in the Mediterranean. Briefly this is what had happened. Already in the thirteenth century merchant ships had become more enterprising, for about the year 1270 Malocello had reached the Canary Isles, and in 1281, Vivaldi had set forth from Genoa to find the East Indies *via* the west coast of Africa, but failed. For you must remember that during the latter part of the twelfth century the compass, crude and inaccurate, yet of immense utility, had been introduced into Europe from the East. Then comes into our story that great man Prince Henry the Navigator, son of the King of Portugal, and nephew of Henry IV of England. Henry devoted his life to developing the science and art of navigation, creating an observatory and nautical school at Sagres, near Cape St. Vincent, and doing all he possibly could to encourage maritime discovery.

The result of this was that the Portuguese became great sea-travellers, big ship-owners and expanded in commerce and colonies. Henry the Navigator was born in 1394 and died in 1460, and to his foresight, organisation and enthusiastic intellect can be traced the rapid and marvellous Portuguese achievements which followed at sea. Thus in 1442 Madeira and the Azores had been discovered in the Atlantic, trade with Africa materially increased, especially on the west coast, and the traffic in black slaves become very profitable.

Then in 1486 the Cape of Good Hope was rounded and the sea

route at last opened to the East Indies, instead of the long and perilous overland route to the Levant which had been used always up till now. In 1498 Vasco da Gama sailed from Lisbon to Calicut, and two years later the Portuguese had landed in Brazil. Thus by the dawn of the sixteenth century Portugal had reached a wonderful height of prosperity. The great Eastern trade was in her hands; Ceylon, the Sunda Islands, Malacca and Ormuz in the Persian Gulf were hers; and all this pre-eminence had been won by studying the problems of the sea and then applying that knowledge in ships manned by practical navigators and sailors.

Portugal had risen up by the twelfth century as a separate kingdom, and Spain had been passing through a period of complete anarchy, but on the death of the Spanish Henry IV, Isabel and Ferdinand had ascended the throne of Castile, and then law and order were restored, the last Moorish stronghold was captured in 1492, and a few months later the Genoese sailor Columbus, under the patronage of Ferdinand and Isabella, was allowed to set forth on his historic voyage which discovered the West Indies. He returned home, went across the Atlantic again in 1493 and discovered Dominica; then made his third voyage, in which he discovered the mainland of South America in 1498, and finally, on his last voyage, explored the southern shore of the Mexican Gulf.

With the discovery of a sea-route both to the East and West Indies, the whole future of the Mercantile Marine was altered. Instead of carrying merchandise and pilgrims across Europe, there came the demand for great ocean-going vessels that could carry home large quantities of rich produce, that would make the European markets surprised when they beheld these goods. Thus the Portuguese and Spaniards, like the Venetians and Genoese, began to amass great wealth from their merchant ships. Noble *caracks* were built, more and more men embarked on a seafaring career, the art of navigation received much more careful study, and mercantile maritime supremacy passed to the Iberian peninsula. Thus the work of great shipbuilders and sea-carriers, discoverers, colonisers and traders had for a time passed into other hands.

But success in one party always breeds jealousy in another: indeed, if you examine the causes of all the great wars in history, or look into the reasons for most private quarrels, you will find usually that they come under the heading either of commercial jealousy or religious intolerance. And when, as was the case in the sixteenth century, you have both these factors united, you have the maximum of intense feeling.

The English seamen, perfectly naturally, began to be jealous and envious of the lectureships and instruction which were being given to these southern seamen. At Seville Charles V had founded a lecture-ship on navigation in the sixteenth century. In England Henry VIII founded three guilds, at Deptford-on-Thames, Kingston-on-Hull and Newcastle-on-Tyne, for the same purpose, and Edward VI selected Sebastian Cabot to be Grand Pilot of England. Henry VII encouraged his shipbuilders by giving them a bounty on the tonnage built, and in Henry VIH's reign dockyards were established at Woolwich, Erith and Deptford, in addition to Portsmouth. Books on the sea arts be-gan to be written in English, so that by the time the full force of the commercial and religious hatred of the Spanish and Portuguese was let loose, the English mercantile mariners were something more than mere coastal seamen.

From their fishing they had gradually become cross-Channel car-riers; from this they had risen to the ability to trade regularly with Spain, with an occasional voyage even to the Mediterranean; but now they were qualified by their ambition and their greater knowledge to go wherever the sea existed. And thus we get Drake going all the way round the world; the many voyages across the Atlantic to the West Indies; the fights with the Spanish treasure ships; the capture of the *Madre de Dios* and *San Felipe*, thus discovering the long-kept secrets of the sea-route to India. From the captured *caracks* and galleons which had been built in the Iberian peninsula, the English shipwright was able to enlarge his ideas and to learn how to build real ocean-going craft bigger than most of the Elizabethan ships.

The introduction of cannon had been an additional reason for making the ship a much stouter, loftier and more formidable creature. Thus length, and beam, and draught increased; larger crews and more officers were needed, and as each expedition came home with strange products, merchant adventurers combined to fit out other expeditions to inaugurate trade even in such remote spots as had not yet seen a white man.

And never a ship came home from her voyage without adding some valuable information in regard to trade or geography or naviga-tion or pilotage. You have only to read the travels in Hakluyt, Purchase and elsewhere to see how keen these Elizabethans were not to omit a single piece of knowledge that would be useful for future voyages.

They had been able, almost suddenly, to realise that, given pluck, determination, enterprise and endurance, the treasures of the world were theirs. They could follow the sea for a few long voyages and then return to build themselves comfortable mansions in Devonshire. And inasmuch as nothing succeeds like success, every time the crew came home and spread the wonderful tales of their experiences and showed the valuables they had managed to obtain, other men were anxious to go forth and do likewise. Nobles and gentlemen and city magnates invested heavily in these trading voyages, selected the ablest seamen, and thus, incidentally, were helping to build up the Mercantile Marine on a grand scale.

Before Hawkins engaged in his trans-Atlantic voyages he was a Plymouth ship-owner accustomed to sail to the ports of Spain and the Canary Islands with trade. At the Canaries he learns a good deal about the West Indies, then goes further south to the west coast of Africa, begins transporting niggers thence to America, returns to England with plenty of money, and sets everyone in the west of England talking and anxious to have a share in this great new game. His relative, Francis Drake, owner of a small brigantine in which coastal trading has been carried on, is fired by Hawkins' success, and accompanies him on one of his expeditions. Young Francis has learnt his seamanship in a rough school, having made friends with a shipmaster trading to the Channel ports and gone to sea with him, and thus acquired his knowledge, until finally the shipmaster dies and leaves him the brigantine in his will. Several years of coastal work had followed, Drake had acquired both money and reputation, and in the end could not resist selling the coaster and buying the brigantine *Judith*, fifty tons, and going with his relative across the Atlantic.

What followed? Every time the English seamen came back with terrible yarns concerning the treachery of the Portuguese and Spaniards, every time the stories of the gallant fights were told, every time the jewels and plate and pearls were seen and handled, the West countrymen were stirred to their very souls. Religious and commercial jealousy, racial hatred and the love of adventure, combined with the possibility of becoming rich—all this created such a fire of enthusiasm that the English Mercantile Marine was bound to increase in numbers and aspirations. The moderate ambitions of the Middle Ages had passed away forever: the dawn of a new order of things had now already come.

CHAPTER 6

The Mercantile Marine
of the Sixteenth Century

By the middle of the fourteenth century the merchant ships had begun to outgrow mediævalism; by the sixteenth they were able to go to windward and to keep the sea for months on end. Thus, vessels had at last begun to enjoy the freedom of the seas and to be independent of the shore. It was a great achievement, considering how limited in size and seaworthiness ships had been, and how limited in knowledge mariners had remained until they had passed through the Middle Ages and emerged into the clear, bright light of science.

Men were getting away from convention and thinking for themselves, but some of the old habits were dying very slowly. One very antique custom was that of waits attending seafaring men. As late as 1466, and probably even after, at the Cinque Ports musicians with fifes and trumpets paraded the town and announced which way the wind was blowing, so that merchant ships could put to sea if the wind was fair for them. The use of the ship's bell had been introduced into Tudor ships before the end of the fifteenth century, for Henry VII's famous *Grâce Dieu* in 1485 included this in her inventory, and the *Regent* in 1495 had two "*wache belles.*"

In a volume printed at the beginning of the sixteenth century, showing a typical merchant ship of the time, with mast, square-sails, and castles from which to attack pirates and other enemies, the artist has actually shown, in a rather conventional, but none the less interesting, manner the skipper at the helm and the merchants with their bales of goods in the vessel; but the pictorial information of these early craft is so slight, and landsmen artists dealing with technical marine subjects were so very inaccurate, that it is only by most diligent and careful research that a nautical student who understands the ways of a ship can follow the development of the merchant craft through to the seventeenth century.

Seamen have very rarely been good authors, until we come to modern times; and writers have usually been unacquainted with the technicalities of seafaring. The difficulty, therefore, has been great. The only solution is to regard the efforts of ancient artists and authors critically with the eyes of a seaman, and to make allowances. With this concession, realising what a ship can do and what she never could be asked to do; realising also that the artist's intention was not so much to bequeath to posterity an accurately rigged ship as to depict an idea—as, for instance, the progress of a saint, in which a ship appeared incidentally—we can find all these quaint artistic efforts worth examining, and yielding up information. So it is with the writers.

Even that fifteenth-century French humorist Rabelais helps us if we allow for his ignorance of seafaring matters. So long as a man writes of what he actually saw with his own eyes, and not what he imagined, we have valuable and illuminative truth. Rabelais was no seaman, but his description of the handling of the ship in a gale is worth preserving.

At the approach of bad weather we see the pilot shortening sail. The terrified Panurge exclaims with horror that the bitts are broken, the tackle is in pieces, the timbers are splitting, the mast dipping into the sea up to the truck. His is the attitude of the "all-is-lost" landsman who exists through all the ages of the merchant ship.

Thus he goes on: "Alas! alas I where are our topsails? All is lost, by God! Our topmast is under water. Alas! to whom will this wreck belong? Friends, put me here behind one of these bulkheads. Lads, your top-crane has fallen."

He hears the rudder-pintle creaking. "Is it broken?"

Eventually the pilot heaves-to under her main-course, but later the weather moderates so that the ship can resume her voyage. "To the main topsail," rings out an order.

"Hoist! hoist! To the main-mizzen topsail. The rope to the capstan. Heave! heave! heave! Hands to the halyards. Hoist! hoist! Clear away the tacks. Clear away the sheets. Clear away the bowlines. Port tack. Down helm. Haul taut starboard sheet. Luff. Full and by. Up helm. ('Up, it is,' replied the sailors.) Keep her going. Head for the harbour-mouth." Thus, with the steering tackles manned, and the ship sailing close-hauled on the port tack, the pilot makes the helmsman keep her out of the wind and straight for their haven. [1]

But those who know their Hakluyt well, and take the trouble to read those wondrous voyages with imagination, are richly rewarded by the interesting sidelights thrown on the sixteenth-century seamanship in the merchant craft. Among the instructions "for the direction of the intended voyage for Cathay," issued by Sebastian Cabot in 1553, the "captain-general," "pilot major," masters, merchants and other officers are first exhorted to be "knit and accorded in unitie, love, conformitie and obedience." Every mariner and passenger took an oath to be obedient to the captain-general, and to every captain and master of his ship. But even as late as the reign of Edward VI, the old custom of the sea, which we have seen in the Mediterranean, prevailed.

The communal idea was not yet extinct. "Item," runs the fifth instruction, "all courses in Navigation to be set and kept, by the advice of the Captaine, Pilot Major, masters, and masters' mates, with the assents of the counsailers and the most number of them, and in voyces uniformely agreeing in one to prevaile, and take place, so that the Captaine generall, shall in all counsailes and assemblies have a double voyce."

The fleet was ordered to keep together, the merchants "and other skilful persons in writing, shal daily write, describe, and put in memorie the Navigation of every day and night, with the points, and observation of the lands, tides, elements, altitude of the sunne, course of the moon and star res, and the same so noted by the order of the Master and pilot of every ship to be put in writing, the captaine generall assembling the masters together once every weeke (if winde and weather shal serve) to conferre all the observations, and notes of the said ships, to the intent it may appeare wherein the notes do agree, and wherein they dissent, and upon good debatement, deliberation, and conclusion determined, to put the same into a common leger, to remain of record for the company: the like order to be kept in proportioning of the Cardes, Astrolabes, and other instruments prepared for the voyage, at the charge of the companie."

Thus the merchants, having financed the voyage, still had a considerable say in the matter. The steward and cook of every ship had to render a weekly account of the flesh, fish, biscuit, meat, bread, beer, wine, oil and vinegar consumed. If an officer or seaman were found inefficient, he could be put ashore anywhere "within the king's Majesties realme and dominion." In order to keep discipline over the

1 *Mariner's Mirror,* Vol. 5. p. 81. 55

crew—many of them the "bad hats" of the port from which the ships had sailed—they were forbidden blasphemy, "ribaldrie, filthy tales or ungodly talke, neither dicing, carding, tabling, nor other divelish games to be frequented, whereby ensueth not onely povertie to the players, but also strife, variance, brauling, fighting, and oftentimes murther."

Every morning and evening, service was to be read in the flagship by "the minister," and in the other ships by the merchant or some other learned person. "No liquor to be spilt on the balast, nor filthines to be left within boord; the cook room, and all other places to be kept cleane, for the better health of the companie."

The merchants were to look after the "liveries in apparel" given to the mariners, which were not to be worn except by order of the captain. And there was also a "slop-chest," taken care of by the merchants, from which a seaman could obtain "any necessarie furniture of apparell for his body, and conservation of his health at such reasonable price as the same cost, without any gaine to be exacted by the marchants." Nor could the merchants exhibit for sale any of their goods to foreigners without consent of the captains and other officers.

In this expedition for the purpose of trading there were three ships, and from these details we have a fair idea of the way the pick of the Mercantile Marine was being conducted on a grand scale, as contrasted with the usual small voyages around the British Isles, or across the North Sea, English Channel and the Bay of Biscay. Such an expedition as the one we are considering aimed at big things: the opening up of a new trade route and fresh markets. Thus there were three ships in this venture, the 120-ton *Bona Esperajiza*, which was the flagship; the 160-ton *Edward Bonaventure*; and the 90-ton *Bona Confidentia*, In the first was Sir Hugh Willoughby, captain-general of the squadron, or, as they called it, the fleet. In that same ship were the master, his mate and six merchants, together with the master gunner, boatswain, boatswain's mate, four quartermasters and their four mates, two carpenters, a purser, a cook and his mate, two surgeons and others.

Two men were landed at Harwich for sickness, and one other was ducked at the yard-arm "for pickerie," and then discharged. The *Edward Bonaventure* carried Richard Chancellor as captain and pilot-major of the fleet, a master, his mate, two merchants, a minister, officers and mariners. The little *Bona Confidentia* carried only a master, his mate, three merchants, as well as the usual officers and mariners. Each of these three ships had a pinnace and a boat. We know that these ships could never lie nearer than seven points from the wind by the statement that "the wind veared to the West, so that we could lie but North and by West." Not having charts of the strange unexplored harbours and havens, the ship, on approaching the land, used to send her pinnace ahead to find an anchorage, and then the big craft could follow in. They used their lead for sounding, and consulted the globe, which was the only knowledge of geography of distant countries possessed in many cases.

But it was no unusual thing to find in these exploratory voyages that "the land lay not as the Globe made mention." In this particular expedition, whereon, by the way. Sir Hugh Willoughby and the company of two of his ships perished in the bitter Lapland regions, there were all sorts of anxieties through gales of winds, leaky ships, shoals, unknown coasts, cold and general discomfort inseparable from crudely built vessels. We can but admire the courageous enter- prise which sent them forth, and thus helped to lay the foundations of our Mercantile Marine and seek a north-east passage to China.

But, as we know from writers of the sixteenth century, the fact was that the commodities and wares of England were in small request with the neighbouring countries. Those goods which, within the memory of the oldest inhabitants, had been in demand, were now neglected, notwithstanding that English ships carried the wares into the harbours of the foreigners. Contrariwise, there was a brisk demand for foreign goods, and at a high price. Therefore certain "grave citizens of London began to thinke with themselves howe this mischiefe might bee remedied."

And observing that the Spaniards and Portuguese had wonderfully increased their wealth by the search and discovery of new countries and trades; and having taken the advice of Sebastian Cabot, who was then in London, these wise merchants formed themselves into a company, and each member put up £25, so that before long the three ships already mentioned were bought and fitted out with the total £6000 thus obtained, and victualled too. These shrewd Edwardians were doing exactly what modern merchants do in a period of trade depression and slump—they went out to look for business in new markets. But the difference was that the former had first to get the ships and then fit them out, instead of merely going to the office of a tourist-agency and purchasing a ticket, and then voyaging in safety, comfort and with the certainty of being in a particular place on a fixed day.

In this north-east expedition, as soon as the money was obtained the merchants bought exceptionally strong and well-seasoned planks, and then the shipwrights set to work with the construction, caulking and pitching them and covering the bottom with lead sheathing. That was all comparatively straight-going, but the difficulty was to victual the ships with food for eighteen months. Indeed, after setting out from the Thames, some of the food by the time they reached Harwich was already putrid and the hogsheads of wine leaking. Ships were ballasted with stones, and before the wind these cumbrous craft would sail well, but on a wind they made a good deal of leeway. But all the time these sixteenth-century mariners were learning, and setting down their records for others to learn.

Thus one finds these pioneers entering such remarks as "a south moone makes a full sea," "Friday I went on shoare and observed the variation of the Compasse, which was three degrees and a halfe from the North to the West; the latitude this day was sixtie nine degrees ten minutes." And in 1557, among the instructions given to masters and mariners of an expedition, it is ordered that notes and entries be daily made of the navigations, and that the young mariners and apprentices be taught and made to learn the same.

Thus, with every voyage north, south, east or west, with every slump or boom in trade, the English Mercantile Marine was becoming more efficient, less unscientific, and the love of seafaring became greater. Those were the great days when, though the ships were of wood, the men's hearts were of gold, and nothing daunted them. Their gear was none too good, their ships were roughly built, and yet no adversity ever overcame their fine spirits. They were ready to struggle with any difficulty. Take the case of the Elizabethan ship which got caught in heavy weather one September. She hove-to, but was washed down by almost every sea, and then the rudder was found to be broken and almost falling off.

Next day, as soon as the weather eased, a dozen of the crew leapt overboard, remained under water as long as possible, worked at the rudder-planking, bound it with ropes, and finally made such a good job of it that it was again serviceable; but by the time they were got aboard once more they were more than half dead. These ships were always losing anchors, cables, boats and *pinnaces*; and even when they had charts and globes, they were finding them full of errors; yet they "kept on keeping on" and bringing their seafaring profession out of the dark recesses of ignorance into the light of knowledge.

Chapter 7

Fishermen and Merchantmen

Up to the end of the sixteenth century we have seen the progress of the Mercantile Marine influenced by the pilgrim and cargo trade in the south of Europe, and in the Iberian peninsula by the long ocean voyages east and west for the purpose of spreading Christianity, trading, and obtaining greater territory. In the north of Europe we have seen that the crusades, as in the south, had their effect, and that pilgrims and merchandise were regularly carried across the Bay of Biscay.

But we have seen, too, that the Hanseatic League and the fishing industry had from early times done much; nor were these influences yet dead. It is interesting, as showing the far-sightedness of the Hanseatics, to note that they were careful to get into their hands the entire corner of hemp, from which ropes were made. Everywhere the League had extended its tentacles as a powerful European trading combine. The market of Bruges was a place where you met all the great travellers and merchants of Europe. Everyone who was any one in commerce sooner or later came here.

In London they had entrenched themselves with characteristic German astuteness, and their privileges had been marvellously protected by the English sovereigns from the twelfth century. Indeed the Hanseatics became, so to speak, the Rothschilds of Europe for financing regal schemes. The Wars of the Roses and the hostilities with France were the means of making the Hanseatics very useful financially, and they got their reward in the shape of special privileges, which their depot just above London Bridge in Thames Street enjoyed for many a year. Down to the time of Edward VI they indeed prospered exceedingly.

In Portugal the League had established a factory at Lisbon, and thence they traded with the Italian commercial republics and also got a hold on the big Levantine trade. But during the reign of Elizabeth Englishmen began to realise their own strength and capabilities at sea. The defeat of the Armada, and the many fights with the Spanish and Portuguese, had given them a confidence which they had never before enjoyed. The English sailors were to justify their maritime ability not merely against the southerners, but against these very powerful and historic members of the northern league.

Consequently they did not hesitate to seize sixty Hanseatic ships about to enter the Tagus with grain for the Spaniards. In 1598 the Hanseatics were turned out of England, and though they were allowed eventually to come back, and their property in the city of London was not sold until 1853, when the Cannon Street railway station was erected, yet the rise of English sea-power, expressed not merely in actual fighting, but in the maritime spirit generally, had given the ancient league its death-blow. Thereafter it merely lingered.

But simultaneously with the decline of the Spanish and Hanseatic Mercantile Marines was growing up the Dutch. And it cannot be emphasised too strongly that this was owing to the herring having in the fifteenth century begun to spawn in the North Sea instead of the Baltic, as already mentioned. It seems curious that an innocent fish should thus be the deciding force of international history. If you examine modern Dutch charts you will still see marked channels and shoals which show the intimate connection which that country had with fishing. The "*haring-vliet,*" or mouth of the Maas, and the "*Schotsman*" shoal, off the island of Walcheren, at once suggest the time when the Low Countries were acquiring wealth by their fisheries and doing a good deal of trade with Scotland. Then they became more ambitious, and built those fine great ships, which you see in the paintings of Vroom and other artists, that were the means of bringing home from their East Indies wealth in another form once enjoyed by the Venetians and Spaniards.

So invaluable had the fisheries been to the Dutch, both in regard to shipbuilding and in creating a fine school of seamanship, that by the time of Cromwell these Netherlanders were the "waggoners of the sea," had the world's carrying trade and owned four-fifths of all the merchant ships that sailed the seas. Now, having regard to the young, keen sea spirit which had made the sixteenth century so illustrious, it was hardly surprising that before long there should be trouble between the English and the Dutch. It was analogous to the years which immediately preceded the Great War of 1914. Collision was certain: it was a question only of time.

Thus, as early as 1608, Grotius, the famous Dutch jurist, wrote his *Mare Liberum*, wherein he contended that the high seas were open to all. Contemporary with him was living the English jurist Selden, who in 1618 had begun his treatise *Mare Clausum*. At the request of James I it was not published for fear of complications with the Danes, but in 1635 Selden again took up this work at the desire of Charles I. In the previous year Charles began to levy ship-money, which really was intended in order to strengthen the fleet against the Dutch in the probability of war.

Legislation is merely the expression of the nation's contemporary fears, and in the long series of maritime Acts from the fourteenth century onwards we can see the national nervousness of the time lest the foreigner should dominate the success of our Mercantile Marine. We have already seen Edward I styling himself "Sovereign of the Seas." Then in the last years of the fourteenth century we have what was the first of the Navigation Acts. The basic aim was to exclude the ships, seamen and trade of the foreigner and to encourage those of our country. We will not bore the reader with a legal dissertation, but it will help us to understand the difficulties of the time if, very briefly, we show how the State was helping the subject of our study.

During the reigns of Henry VII, Henry VIII and Elizabeth there was legislation dealing with the privileges of English shipping. At a later date the claim to the sovereignty of the seas was expressed by compelling the Flemish subjects of Philip, who married our Queen Mary, to pay a fine and an annual rent of £1000 for twenty-one years' lease of the fishing near the north Irish coast, whilst a similar lease with similar conditions was granted by Mary to the Hanseatics. Without a licence foreign subjects were forbidden to fish in English waters, though with the decline of English sea-power in the seventeenth century foreigners ceased to be bound by these claims.

The doctrine of the "Dominion of the Seas" inseparably bound up in the growth of our Mercantile Marine and our fishing industry. Matters reach a crisis in the dispute, and then the discussion is settled by an appeal to force in the shape of war. The Anglo-Dutch wars were fundamentally caused by the herring fisheries and the Mercantile Marines of the two nations. Every other reason was entirely artificial and subservient. Whether the seas could be free to all everywhere to trade, whether the fisherman could shoot his nets where he liked—that is the whole matter in a nutshell. And the more ships that were built for trade or fishing, the more serious the crisis developed. Proportionately the value of a navy becomes greater, and thus the two services are bound to become less and less similar, as greater commercial demands are made on the one and purely warlike requirements are insisted on for the other.

The seventeenth century was the crisis in the career of the Mercantile Marine, for it was struggling for its very life amid many dangers, but it emerged with an independence and character of its own. In any long period of assured peace it reaches enormous heights of success, as, for instance, during the nineteenth century. But during the Caroline period a principle was being insisted upon. The position was this. Charles I was determined to compel the Dutch to acknowledge the English claim to the dominion of the seas, and that was the reason for the building, in 1637, of that marvellous and sensational warship the *Sovereign of the Seas*, a triumph of Pett's design, which Van der Velde depicted for posterity. This 1683-ton "battle-ship," as we should call her nowadays, was an expression, both in name and character, of the English attitude in regard to the use of the seas.

"We hold it a principle," Charles had instructed his Minister at The Hague, "not to be denied, that the King of Great Britain is a monarch at sea and on land to the full extent of his dominions. His Majesty finds it necessary for his own defence and safety to reassume and keep his ancient and undoubted rights in the Dominion of the Seas." Having forbidden foreigners to fish off our coasts without licence, Charles' fleet attacked and put to flight a Dutch fishing fleet which had infringed this order. Some of these small craft were thus sunk by our men-of-war, and many of the rest took shelter in harbour. Finally the Dutch agreed to pay Charles I £30,000 for permission to finish that year's fishing, and to pay a sum annually for the like privilege.

We can well understand the irritation which this line of action caused so great a maritime power as the Dutch. Great sea pioneers they certainly were, and before the first decade after the defeat of the Armada had passed, they had been the first country to send out a real Polar expedition. In 1651 came the celebrated English Navigation Act, which prohibited the importation of goods into England except in English ships, or in the ships of the country producing the goods. This was quite obviously aimed at the great Dutch sea-carriers. Relations became strained, the war-clouds gathered, and in the following year the first of the three Anglo-Dutch wars broke out inevitably between the English and Dutch republics.

The Navigation Act of 1651 was confirmed by that of nine years later, and thus the English Mercantile Marine had its future settled on sure foundations. In a word, the disputes as to where fishermen could shoot their nets to get herrings were the indirect means of giving the merchant ships their unique opportunity. Holland's carrying trade fell into our hands, prosperity came to our country, the sailing ships of our nation penetrated everywhere, and, as you can see by the seventeenth-century architecture in the leading Dutch cities, the wealth obtained overseas suddenly ceased to flow in a big way. It is for those who have eyes a veritable story in stones, which ends suddenly and dramatically.

It is to the credit of the rulers of our country in the seventeenth century that they realised what the fisheries meant to us. The Act of 1651 was of great assistance in providing that no fish should be brought into England or Ireland, or exported thence to foreign parts, or even carried from one English or Irish port to another, except fish caught by English and Irish fishermen in English and Irish ships. In 1661 the Parliament of Scotland also passed navigation laws for the encouragement of their native shipping, and one Act for founding companies to extend the fishing industry. Very subtle, too, was the proclamation of James I in 1621 against eating flesh in Lent or on other "fish days," the reasons given being "the maintenance of our navy and shipping, a principal strength of this island, and for the sparing and increase of fresh victuals." This and similar proclamations considerably helped the fishermen.

In order fully to appreciate all that the fishing meant to the Dutch, it is necessary to mention also that not merely did they seek the herring as far away as the Thames estuary, the Orkneys, Shetlands and the Irish coast, but, owing to the ingenuity and enterprise of one Beuckels, they had learned how to cure and barrel this fish. In this way they enjoyed a wonderful monopoly in supplying Catholic central and northern Europe. In the year 1560, for instance, the value of the year's fishing trade to Friesland, Holland, Zeeland and Flanders amounted to the enormous sum of £300,000. Just as today the steam fish-carriers go out to fetch the catch home from the fleets fishing off the Dogger Bank and elsewhere, so the Dutch in the seventeenth century were using a fast-sailing type of craft, called "*vent-jagers*," to hurry into port the fresh herrings caught by the slow, round, tubby "busses." This practice was in vogue certainly by 1604.

It was a statute of 1663, for the encouragement of our fisheries, which forbade any fresh herrings being imported into England except in English-built ships, and no ship could sail for Iceland from England until March 10, thus protecting the fish at breeding time.

The Act of 1666 prohibited the importation of herrings caught by foreigners. And, having done all this, the time came when those Englishmen who owned capital thought they saw an opportunity for getting richer. Thus in 1677 a Royal Fishery Company was incorporated, the Duke of York and many peers and gentlemen being partners, with a capital eventually increased to £12,580. This was spent in the construction of seven busses, but some of these were captured by the French, who were now growing up as maritime and commercial people, and were rivals to us in our fishing. The remainder of the busses were sold off in 1680 and the company ended in debt.

Three years later another fishing company was started, and this failed also, whereas the Dutch were doing well with their nets, employing 8000 vessels and 200,000 hands, thus amassing the enormous sum of £5,000,000 a year. During the time of Charles II the Dutch fishermen had brought great prosperity to Great Yarmouth, sometimes as many as 1000 busses and fish-carriers being off that port, and buying bread, beer, flesh and butter from the East Anglians. They used to come ashore and dry their nets, and the town would find 10,000 of these foreign sailor-men in their neighbourhood. To assuage their thirst, forty brewers were kept busy in the port. Anyone who has any experience of human nature and of fishermen, will readily understand that there were many feuds and quarrellings. Ever since 1540 the Dutchmen had been herring-fishing off that port, and the Englishmen were none too pleased at this visitation; nor were the Scotch, who in 1532 attacked the Dutchmen and captured many of their busses, and for nine years prevented them from using Scottish waters.

As far back as the thirteenth century the herring had been caught in great numbers off Great Yarmouth, and in 1270 the Yarmouth herring fair was held for forty days. About that date some Flemish vessels put to sea and killed 1200 English North Sea fishermen, nor will these international fishermen's quarrels ever cease as long as human nature remains what it is. Before the end of the thirteenth century Grimsby had begun fishing, and before the end of the sixteenth century the first Hull whaler had started out on her special industry, whaling having begun in England only four years previously. Few people are more conservative than the sailor, and of his service the most conservative of all is the fisherman, who did not take to steam generally for many a long year after it had become dominant in the carrying trade.

Many of us can still remember the famous "blue" sailing fishing fleet out of Great Yarmouth; and the Brixham fleet and others round our coasts still stick almost exclusively to sail. In the olden days, wool, wheat, fish and other cargoes were sold by the "last." Wool is no longer thus sold, but a hundred years ago wheat was thus reckoned at Great Yarmouth, and round our coasts to this day fish is still disposed of in the old-time manner, a Yarmouth "last" amounting roughly to 13,200 herrings or about two and a half tons.

In our British North Sea fishing craft the busses have given way very largely to steam drifters, but off the Dutch shores the Scheveningen "pink" is much the same craft in hull as were the vessels which caused so much friction in the seventeenth century. The very word by which these craft have been known is in itself symbolical of the antiquity of the industry. The mediæval Venetians had "*buzi*," and throughout the Romance and Teutonic languages it has always meant a fishing boat, the seventeenth century Englishmen getting the use from the Dutch North Sea craft.

The two principal types of fishing craft in the North Sea were the *buss* and the "*dogger*." With regard to the former, the earliest illustration I have discovered is that by Elandts in the Municipal Museum at The Hague, made in 1664 from a picture of 1570. This "baring buys" is the prototype of the seventeenth century buss, and consists of two masts, each having a square-sail. Like the modern drifter, the *buss* lowered her foremast and rode to her nets. This Elandts *buss* is really nothing more than a large open boat, with three hands in her; the length of the craft I reckon not more than about thirty feet.

A rather bigger type, similarly rigged but with three masts, is depicted in the Dutch Waghenaer's *Speculum Nauticum* of 1584 riding to her nets, with fore and mainmasts lowered. Among the sixteen ships which Frobisher took with him in 1578, one was the Emmanuel of Bridgewater, and she is described as a *buss*. It will be recollected that this was another attempt to find the north-west passage to China, and this craft performed most admirable service, and as she came homeward discovered an island which had never before been sighted. Thus, there is no question about the seaworthiness of this fishing type of craft.

In the Boijmans Museum, Rotterdam, there is an interesting painting by Bellevois showing a mid-seventeenth century *buss* of a powerful type, with three masts, a square-sail on each, and riding with her mizzen up, but the other sails and masts lowered. Keymor, who wrote in 1601 on the Dutch fishing, describes these craft as being from sixty to two hundred tons, and carrying from forty to a hundred lasts. The anonymous author of *Britaine's Busse*, published in 1615, describes them as being of from thirty-five lasts or seventy tons, and measuring fifty feet on the keel, with a beam of seventeen feet. Her cost, together with her boat, was £260. There is another fine picture of these craft by Storck, hanging in the Mauritshuis at The Hague, the date being 1683, and from the rounded stern and general lines of the ship it is easy enough to see that she belongs to the same family to which the familiar Scheveningen "pink," so well known in modern art, belongs.

Often in the mediæval records one finds reference to a North Sea fishing type called the "*dogger*." Exactly what these were like, it would be impossible to say, except that they probably had not more than two masts carrying square sails, and that they were line fishers, for cod and ling, and did not use nets, their size in the seventeenth century varying from sixty to one hundred tons. It is reasonable to suppose, from the later illustrations which exist, that the *dogger* was in hull and square-sails not very different from the *buss*.

The end of the seventeenth century, then, saw the British Mercantile Marine both in respect of its fishing craft and its cargo-carriers, going ahead. As regards the latter, the finest of all were the ships of the East India Company of England and those of the Dutch East India Company, with their stately hulls, lofty sterns, high freeboard and two decks of guns. A picture of 1647 shows them with three masts, as well as bowsprit, and they even carry topgallant sails on fore and main. Such craft are, in fact, the connecting link between the last of the mediaeval ships and the first of the famous clipper ships.

The stolid majesty of their design and build, the elaborateness of their seventeenth century carvings, were expressive of that permanence with which the Merchant Service now rightly regarded itself. Indeed so prosperous had the British East India Company become in the seventeenth century, that by 1681 this corporation owned about thirty-five ships, ranging in size from 100 to 775 tons, and in customs alone the company was paying £60,000 a year. They used to take out to India cargoes of lead, tin, cloth and stuffs, bringing back home raw silk, pepper and other Eastern goods. Trade prospered so well, indeed, that between 1682 and 1689 as many as sixteen East Indiamen of from 900 to 1300 tons were built, and all these ships had to be armed; for during the last decade of that century these merchantmen ran the risk of being attacked by French men-of-war as well as by privateers, so that in carrying from thirty to fifty guns these East Indiamen were very powerful vessels for any enemy to have to encounter.

SEVENTEENTH–CENTURY DUTCH EAST INDIAMEN

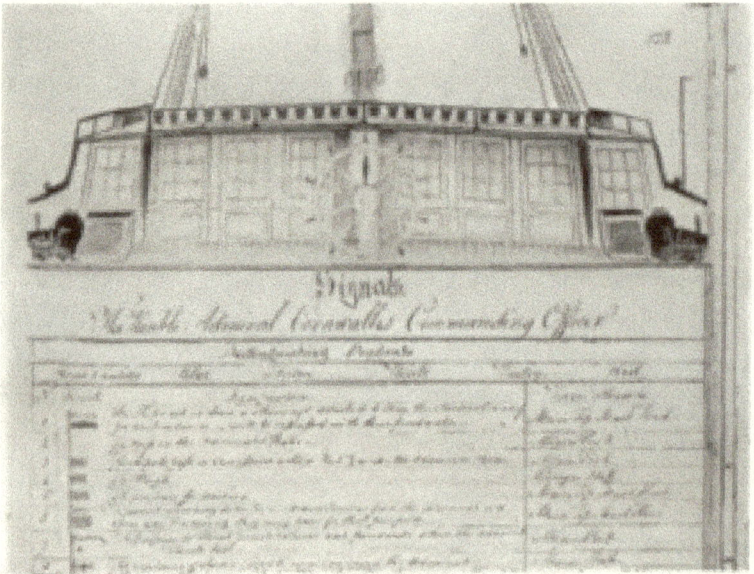

SIGNAL CODES.

CHAPTER 8

Seventeenth Century Seafaring

Few people realise that the trade routes of the world are the lanes along which history is constrained to flow. It is a fascinating study, but we have little enough room to develop the subject here. The success of Prince Henry the Navigator's influence, the achievement of Vasco da Gama, completely revolutionised the trade routes of the world, transformed the European mercantile system, made the gate of commerce not Venice but Lisbon, transferred the centre of progress from the Mediterranean to the Atlantic; and the discovery of America accentuated this new condition still further.

What followed? First, the Dutch, having built up a shipping industry, so to speak, on the backbone of the herring, were able to get the trade of distributing these goods from Lisbon to the north European countries. This, in turn, caused competition on the part of the English, who were not intending to be left out of the new fortune. Secondly, the Dutch and English began themselves to voyage to the East. And thirdly, the discovery of the rich possibilities of the East and West not merely made the Mediterranean commercially of little future account, but gave to the nations of the European Atlantic coasts an impetus to progress and a reason for strife which had never yet occurred. The history of the seventeenth to the twentieth centuries is confined to the struggle for the dominion of the seas—that is, maritime commercial supremacy, caused by the flow of trade taking a new route. The wars with the Dutch, the French and the Spanish were at heart the struggle for possession of overseas commerce, and the recent war with Germany was animated by the same cause.

It is impossible to emphasise this trade-route influence too much, for without a clear appreciation of its place in history the sequence of events becomes meaningless, and the rise and development of the

Mercantile Marine seem arbitrary. Prince Henry the Navigator started a wonderful sea contest, and it has never stopped during the ensuing centuries. As soon as one keen competitor drops out, another comes in to keep up the running. That has been the impelling influence in the history of the English Mercantile Marine. When Spain falls out, the Dutch take her place. When they cease to be competitors, the French become the pacemakers, to be followed by the Germans; and now that the latter have disappeared almost entirely from the sea, the United States ships of commerce will maintain this ancient contest. And so it will go on, unless air routes cause another revolution in the transport of merchandise, and give another sudden twist to the flow of history.

The seventeenth century, then, saw a wonderful incentive to the English Merchant Navy just because the East was calling. And, as a result of this, there followed in due succession the creation of the East India Company, the wonderful and famous East Indiamen built chiefly at Blackwall; then, after the long monopoly came to an end, the famous Blackwall sailing ships of the Wigrams and Greens, the historic clippers, and finally the Peninsular and Oriental Steam Navigation Company.

From the year 1582 for the next three hundred years from Blackwall, on the River Thames, sailing ships year after year made their way to the Orient, and it is to my mind one of the most remarkable continuities in the history of human things. It is certainly one of the most, if not the most, critical of periods in the development of the commercial marine. What Portsmouth has been to the British navy, the village of Blackwall has been to the British Mercantile Marine. From the Blackwall yard were launched hundreds of East Indiamen; from here came improved and novel designs for the sailing ships that were to win and retain against all competitors commercial supremacy at sea for the British nation. But for these craft the trend of English history, of the world's history, would be entirely different.

There would have been neither the cause nor the means of a powerful navy; nor of Colonial expansion; nor would the position which Britain possesses financially have been possible. I am omitting intentionally for the present the development of the American trade, for that came later. It was the Eastern overseas trade in the merchant ships of the seventeenth, eighteenth and nineteenth centuries which was responsible for an enormous part of the national wealth, many of our costliest buildings and institutions, the founding of illustrious families, and indirectly the awakening of Japan. All this dates back to Prince Henry and Vasco da Gama—to the finding of a sea route to the East.

It was in April 1582 that the first ship left for the East—when the *Edward Bonaventure* sailed from Black wall, joined the flagship *Leicester* at Southampton, and, four weeks out from the London river, accompanied the two other ships. They made a futile attempt to reach India west about, and because the Spanish Fleet were in the neighbourhood of the Magellan Straits, had to return to England. In 1595 Holland sent four ships round the Cape of Good Hope, and two years later the expedition came back, after making a treaty with the King of Bantam and thus opening up the Indian archipelago. In 1599 a number of merchants in London petitioned Elizabeth for permission to have a monopoly to trade with the East Indies, and on the last day of the following year this privilege was granted for fifteen years, and thus the first East India Company began.

A small squadron of ships left the Thames in 1601 with iron, lead, tin and presents for the Indian princes, doubled the Cape of Good Hope on November 1, and reached Sumatra on June 5, 1602. By September 11, 1603, the flagship *Red Dragon* anchored in the Downs, after a most successful voyage, bringing home 1,080,000 lbs. of pepper in the four ships. And thus the beginning of Anglo-Indian commerce started so profitably that matters went ahead. The monopoly was extended and prolonged, until as a fact it was not abrogated until 1833. Expedition after expedition was sent out, until it became the normal routine; the ships of the East India Company were a kind of bridge between the Thames and the Orient. The Merchant Navy was thus on the way to becoming something different from the fighting service, though it was not until many years had passed, not until wars had ceased, privateers and pirates had ended their activities, that the former could afford to give up mounting guns and carrying gunners.

Nineteenth century peace thus gave a basis for separating the two types of ships and the two kinds of personnel; and thereafter the Royal Navy and the Mercantile Marine developed on divergent lines. But, up to that stage, the East Indiaman differed little enough from many of her contemporary men–of–war. Although formally the separation came earlier, it is from after 1815 that the real separation takes place, and the amalgamation never occurred again for a hundred years, when, temporarily, the ships and men of the Merchant Service came to join up with the Royal Navy as fighting units during the Great War.

We need not follow in detail the events of the great East India

Company's rule—by far the most extraordinary monopoly which Europe has ever had with an overseas country. It is important, however, to note the effect of this in stimulating shipping affairs. The Dutch and English began to improve their ships as well they might for so long an ocean voyage.

As to the former, the picture galleries in such places as Middelburg, and Rotterdam, and Amsterdam show what truly magnificent craft they were, with their t'gallant-sails, high poops, stern galleries and ornate decoration. They were the embodiment of wealth. In the first decade of the seventeenth century there was built in England the *Trades Increase,* for the English Company's Indian trade. She was of about 1100 tons burthen, and was the biggest merchant ship which had ever been built in this country. But she was really too big for the knowledge of naval architecture then existing. Clumsy, unwieldy and top-heavy, she got out to the East, but at Bantam, whilst she was being careened to have her sheathing examined, she fell over on to her side and became a total loss, the date being 1613.

Nevertheless, shipbuilding did receive a great stimulus, and this growing interest caused the formation of the Shipwrights Company, its incorporation taking place in 1612; Phineas Pett, whose family for two hundred years had been the greatest English naval architects, becoming its first master. By this date of 1612 the yard at Blackwall, which was to be during the next two and a half centuries so famous, was already well established, and twenty years later almshouses were established at Poplar for invalided petty officers of the East India Company's ships.

For when we think of the Merchant Service in England during the seventeenth and eighteenth centuries, it is almost exclusively of the East Indiamen. It begins gradually, and becomes more important as time goes on and the grip on the East gets tighter. The great port was London, for it was not until the opening up of the trade with America in 1756 that Liverpool began in any way to compete as a great shipping centre, though actually it was not until 1815 that the Lancashire port made great strides. Nevertheless we must not get a false impression. The Tudor awakening had created comparatively few big ships, and even in 1615 there were only ten craft of more than 200 tons burthen belonging to the Port of London. Still, it was the eve of brilliant developments, the like of which the world had never before known. Though they could not have foreseen it, the Blackwall shipwrights were preparing the way for the coming of the most perfect sailing ships which the world has ever seen, or probably ever will see—the clippers of the mid-nineteenth century.

In 1661 Pepys goes by barge to the Blackwall yard to see the new wet dock, the largest in England, and the "brave new merchantman *Royal Oake*," which was nearly ready for launching. In the following year Evelyn refers to accompanying the Duke of York to an East India vessel at Blackwall, and going aboard her where they drank punch and "canary that had been carried to and brought from the Indies, which was indeed incomparably good."

But before the East India Company had offices in the Blackwall yard and superintended the building of its ships, they had a yard of their own at Deptford. This dates from the year 1607, where they soon found employment for five hundred carpenters, caulkers, joiners, and others. Here there existed a wonderful organisation; large stocks of timber, masts, yards, canvas, and other stores. There were such officials as the ship's husband, the clerk of the stores, the buyers, the clerk of the yard, the master shipwright, the master pilot (who had to survey the ships both here and at Blackwall), the boatswain-general, treasurers, purser-general, the clerk of the cordage, the surgeon-general, clerk of the slaughter-house (to look after the victuals), and so on. It was a hive of great activity, and by the year 1621 they had built so many ships that the company owned 10,000 tons of shipping. They had exported from England in their vessels £319,211 worth of woollen goods, lead, iron, tin and other commodities, and had brought home from the East £375,288 worth of cargoes, which were sold in England for the immense sum of £2,044,600. The average profit made by the first twelve voyages amounted to not less than 138 *per cent.*

But after leasing the Deptford yard for twenty years, it was found to be so costly that it swallowed up too much of the capital, which could be employed more profitably in hiring ships. Therefore the Blackwall yard became responsible for the building of practically all the East Indiamen. The company went on from prosperity to wealth. In 1681 they owned thirty-five ships of from 100 to 775 tons, and two years later a £100 share would sell for £500. In 1667 was imported the first cargo of tea, which in the nineteenth century was to be the means of bringing into existence those wonderful tea-clippers.

And now let us see something of the kind of existence which the merchant sailor led during the seventeenth century. He and his mode of life were regarded by the landsman as something strange, something abnormal. Contrariwise, the sailor realised that his art was almost beyond the landsman's comprehension. That spirit, even in this twentieth century, is anything but dead, and between the two avocations there must always exist a big gulf. But we have to remember that in the seventeenth century seafaring was still such a modern and rare career (though yearly increasing in popularity) that he who made a profession of it was an unusual being.

"The sea language," wrote the seventeenth-century Sir William Monson in his Naval Tracts, "is not soon learned, much less understood . . . a boisterous sea and stormy weather will make a man not bred on it so sick, that it bereaves him of legs and stomach and courage . . . when he hears the seamen cry starboard, or port, or to bide aloof, or flat a sheet, or haul home a cluling, he thinks he hears a barbarous speech, which he conceives not the meaning of."

Similarly John Lyly, the dramatist who died in 1606, in his *Gallathea*, gives a dialogue between a mariner and three sons of a miller in which this difference is indicated. The landsmen will never go to sea again, for the bread is hard and the meat salt, and the mariner is pitied for being "pinned in a few boards, and . . . within an inch of a thing bottomless."

The mariner, however, rather delights in showing his superiority over them. "I can shift the moon and the sun," he exclaims, "the lodestone that always holdeth his nose to the North, the two and thirty points for the wind, the wonders I see—would make you blind. You be but boys. I fear the sea no more than a dish of water."

He then tries to teach them the points of the compass, but they cannot learn them. "O dullard," he remarks in disgust, "is thy head lighter than the wind, and thy tongue so heavy it will not wag?"

Richard Braithwait, who wrote during the seventeenth century, published in 1631, in his *Whimzies* an essay on the contemporary sailor, whom he admires for his pluck, disregard of danger and for his hardihood. He looks upon him as a desperate, hearty good-natured fellow of dissolute habits when ashore.

The bredth of an inch-boord is betwixt him and drowning, yet hee swears and drinks as deeply as if hee were a fathom from it. . . . Hee is most constant to his shirt, and other his seldome wash'd linnen. . . . What a starveling hee is in a frosty morning, with his Sea frocke, which seems as it were shrunke from him, and growne too short, but it will be long enough ere hee get another.

The English writer Sir Thomas Overbury, who was arrested and confined in the Tower, and died in 1613, has left behind a study of the character of the sailor at this time. He wittily describes him as :

.. a pitched piece of reason, caulked and tackled, and only studied to dispute with tempests. . . . A fair wind is the substance of his creed, and fresh water the burden of his prayers. . . . In a storm 'tis disputable whether the noise be more his or the elements', and which will first leave scolding. . . . His language is a new confusion, and all his thoughts new nations. His body and his ship are both one burden. Nor is it known who stows most wine, or rolls most—only the ship is guided.

The references to life at sea in the seventeenth century merchantmen are not many, but here and there one comes across mention of some ship or experience. Pepys, whilst sailing down the Thames estuary on Sunday, April 8, 1660, writes in his diary:

"We had a brave wind all the afternoon, and overtook two merchantmen that overtook us yesterday, going to the East Indies."

But there are two interesting passages in English literature which show that going to sea in the ships of this period was a terrible business. The first is found in the autobiography of Edward, Lord Herbert of Cherbury, an English historian and diplomatist, who describes his experience of crossing the English Channel in a French ship in the year 1609. The second is taken from Jonathan Swift's famous *Gulliver's Travels*. There is no need to ask why fiction should be dragged into history; for Swift borrowed this descriptive account of an East Indiaman in a storm almost word for word from James Love's *The Mariner's Jewels* and it gives us a glimpse into the seafaring of the beginning of the eighteenth century that bears the stamp of authenticity. And it is such peeps into the past that are so invaluable to us in reconstructing the life led by the rough seaman at this time, who was learning by his mistakes, risking much by his ignorance, but doing so much for the great Merchant Service that was to spread all over the world.

Herbert, together with Sir Thomas Lucy returning from France, took ship from Dieppe early in February and spent the night in the Channel during a gale of wind.

"The master of our ship," he wrote, "lost both the use of his compass and his reason. For, not knowing whither he was carried by the tempest, all the help he had was by the lightnings, which, together with thunder very frequently that night, terrified him, yet gave the advantage sometimes to discover whether we were upon our coast to which he thought, by the course of his glasses, we were near approached."

That is to say, the master was anxious about his dead reckoning, which was kept by guessing the distance run every hour. The time was kept by means of hourly and half-hourly glasses from Elizabethan times even to the eighteenth century aboard ship, according to the number of times the sand ran through.

Towards daylight the ship sighted Dover and the master made for it. Here the local seafarers were in great numbers by the shore on the lookout for wreckage, for the gale had blown down their own barns and trees. But the French skipper was either a very bad seaman, or his ship was extremely unhandy, for the craft went smack up against Dover pier and split, whereupon the Frenchman cheerfully announced: "*Mes amis, nous sommes perdus.*" Herbert, though in the toils of seasickness, then emerged from his cabin, climbed part of the way up the mast and waved his sword for help. A local six-oared boat then came off, into which Herbert was the first to enter. Lucy was half dead with sea-sickness, but was lifted from the cabin to the boat, and thus they were saved. Other boats rowed off the rest of the men and the horses. The ship, concluded Herbert, "was wholly split and cast away, insomuch that in pity to the master, Sir Thomas Lucy and myself gave thirty pounds towards his loss, which yet was not so great as we thought, since the tide now ebbing, he recovered the broken parts of his ship."

Dean Swift, in *Gulliver's Travels*, refers to the ship *Adventure* riding in the Downs at the end of June 1702. She was commanded by Captain John Nicholas, a Cornishman, and bound for Surat. At the Cape of Good Hope they landed for fresh water, but other reasons detained them until the end of March. A good passage was then made till north of Madagascar, when bad weather was encountered. The spritsail (the square-sail set on a small mast at the end of the bowsprit) was therefore taken in, the mizzen was handed, and the guns secured. Rather than heave-to, the captain decided to run before the wind—"spooning" is the technical expression—the foresail was reefed, the fore-sheet hauled aft, the helm put hard aweather, and "the ship wore bravely." But the foresail became split, and the yard was hauled down. "It was a very fierce storm; the sea broke strange and dangerous. We hauled off upon the lanyard of the whip-staff, and helped the man at helm." For there was no steering wheel in use yet, and this was not introduced until about fifty years later. The tiller from the rudder was controlled by a vertical bar or lever, called a "whip-staff," and the lanyards would naturally enough be used, as it is employed to this day for assisting the helm of sailing yachts.

After scudding before the storm, the weather at last eased up. Then the ship set her foresail and mainsail and hove-to, and finally set the mizzen, main-topsail and fore-topsail, and with the wind S.W. ran a course E.N.E. Then they "got the starboard tacks aboard" and headed S.S.E. " We cast off our weather braces and lifts. We set in the lee braces and hauled forward by the weather bowlines and hauled them tight and belayed them, and hauled over the mizzen tack to windward and kept her full-and-by as near as she could lie." That is to say, the ship was now trimmed to sail on a wind, the bowlines, which were connected by bridles to the leech of the sail, being used to keep the weather edge well hauled out tight, to make the canvas set properly. The mizzen, of course, was still a triangular, fore and aft sail. Finally on June 3, 1703, a boy on the topmast sighted land.

It is a little difficult in this highly specialised twentieth century to appreciate the slight difference which existed between a merchant ship and a man-of-war. Between the men of the Merchant Service and those of the Navy there was thus little to choose. From the Elizabethan days most merchant ships of any size had to be armed for their own defence. Moreover the merchantman was as much privateer or pirate as he was freighter. He had to be a fighting man, whatever else he might be. Thus there was always at hand a reserve of crews which could be "imprest" into the Navy. During the first quarter of the seventeenth century the merchants were paying their crews thirty shillings a month, whilst the men in the Royal ships were receiving less than half this amount. The result was that for a time the merchant ships attracted the best seamen.

It was from the Merchant Service that some of the most distinguished officers of the Royal Navy graduated. Admiral Benbow, for instance, had been an apprentice in the Merchant Service, and was eventually given command of a naval ship such as was usually given to a lieutenant. He was promoted later to captain and to flag rank. This caused jealousy and bad feeling, and the reader will remember that this Admiral, when attacking the enemy in 1702 in the West Indies, was basely deserted by some of his captains, but he carried on a running fight almost singlehanded for five days.

Other names could be mentioned, too. Neither masters nor mates were exempt from being impressed; and these rough, daring merchantmen, who fought as hard as they drank, who despised the enemy as heartily as they despised cowardice, were the very life-blood of the nation that was growing up to prosperous adolescence. England was just realising what was the meaning of the word sea. As Francis Bacon wrote in his essay:

> To be master of the sea is an abridgment of a monarchy. . . . Surely, at this day, with us of Europe, the vantage of strength at sea (which is one of the principal dowries of this kingdom of Great Britain) is great; both because most of the kingdoms of Europe are not merely inland, but girt with the sea most part of their compass; and because the wealth of both Indies seems in great part but an accessory to the command of the seas.

It takes time for a nation to appreciate all that maritime progress connotes. We in this twentieth century have seen that it required the Great European War to enable the United States to realise this, and the present American mercantile shipping activity and development are the practical results of this appreciation. The Merchant Navy to a country is the basis on which her fighting navy is built. It is the avenue along which her commerce must flow out and home.

CHAPTER 9

Mercantile Supremacy at Sea

The end of the seventeenth century saw the British Mercantile Fleet as the world's leading traders. The disappearance of their Spanish and then Dutch rivals in sea commerce was brought about not by battle, but by the steady pressure of sea-power, as in the recent European War the continuous pressure of the Grand Fleet throttled the Germans. Just as the Battle of Jutland failed to bring about the downfall of our late enemies, so the defeat of the Armada did not succeed in breaking Spain; so too, no single battle in the Anglo-Dutch wars brought the maritime progress of the great Dutch Republic to a dead stop.

This sea pressure having fulfilled its purpose, the English merchantmen were able to scoop up from exhausted nations the world's maritime commerce; and the voyages of discovery, notably those of Dampier, Anson and Cook, together with the enterprising penetration of the East Indiamen, and to a smaller extent the West Indiamen (who enjoyed the benefits of free trade), opened up fresh avenues of commerce. The fighting fleers had opened up the oceans for the mercantile ships to bring home riches. By the year 1688 the annual clearance outwards from Great Britain was 191,000 tons of English shipping and 95,000 tons of foreign shipping. In a hundred years the nation had become supreme, simply because our forefathers, like any great business man, had possessed the imagination to see that the ocean was the road to wealth, and they had also not lacked the courage to put their maritime belief to the test.

Thus in the year 1701-1702 its Mercantile Marine consisted of 3281 vessels of 261,222 tons, armed with 5660 guns and giving employment afloat to 27,196 men. During the eighteenth century wet docks had to be made both in the Thames and the Mersey, the first

CAPTAIN THOMAS FORREST. NAVIGATOR AND SURVEYOR, WHO
FORMED IN 1770 FOR THE H.E. INDIA COMPANY
A NEW SETTLEMENT AT BALAMBANGAN.

Marine Insurance Company came into being, and Lloyd's Register of Shipping was started. The history of Lloyd's is indicative of the progress of the Mercantile Marine. In the seventeenth century a number of underwriters used to meet in Edward Lloyd's coffee-house in Tower Street for their business. In 1692 this coffee-house was removed to Lombard Street, and then, in 1774, Lloyd's gave up the coffee-house and went to their premises in the Royal Exchange, where they have remained ever since.

It is clear from Lloyd's Register of Shipping that from 1764 to the end of that century most of the British ships were of not more than 300 tons; but we have to bear in mind two important facts. Firstly, the East Indian monopoly prevented competition, and therefore any stimulus to build anything larger; and secondly, from 1775 to 1815, with only small patches of peace, there was a long series of wars. These hostilities naturally caused the tonnage of commercial shipping to drop, but every time that peace was restored the figures began to go up again; so that in 1793, when war broke out with France, Great Britain possessed 16,079 merchant ships as compared with the 3281 at the commencement of the century. It was therefore an amazingly live industry, which required only a fair opportunity for its development.

This development was, as might be expected, accurately reflected at the Blackwall yard, in spite of the fact that the slips and shipwrights had largely during those forty years to be employed for building men-of-war for the Navy. By the middle of the century this yard had a wet dock, three dry docks and a number of slips. It was the biggest private dockyard in the country, and only the Royal yards could rival it. Here the East Indiamen continued to be built, the direct ancestors of the great liners of today. In the period 1750-1752 was here constructed the East Indiaman *Falmouth*. She was a fine three-masted, full-rigged ship of 668 tons burthen, measuring 108 feet 9 inches on the keel, and having a beam of 34 feet. She carried topsails and t'gallant sails and, with her large figure-head and rather wasteful, ornate design at bow and stern, maintained her close connection with the ship architecture of the seventeenth century.

During the next thirteen years were launched such East Indiamen as the 642-ton *Osterley*, the 642-ton *Tilbury*, the *Valentine* and *Ajax*, each of 655 tons. In 1763 no fewer than five such ships of 670 tons were constructed and fitted out, and then, a couple of years later, ships of 700 tons began to be built. The East India Company used to charter such ships practically as long as they were seaworthy; and Blackwall in those days was able to do everything that the monopolists required; for here not only were the ships built, rigged and laid up, but ashore the houses were the homes of seafaring families, shipwrights, caulkers and every trade concerned in the building of these craft. And then in 1789 was launched from this yard the big 1612-ton *Bombay Castle*, a powerful vessel of seventy-four guns, which the East India Company presented to George III. There is a picture by Dodd which shows as many as four other big ships on the slips at this time, together with four or five similar craft fitting out in the stream. It is comparable only to the Clyde in the height of its twentieth-century shipbuilding.

With the increase in the number of these ships came, of course, the greater need for docks where the vessels could lie in tiers in safety and convenience; so in 1789 the Brunswick Basin was begun in the east end of the Blackwall yard. Two years later the first ship was masted here. This was the *Lord Macartney*, and you may guess of the keenness and smartness of the men when you learn that her bowsprit and all her masts were raised and fixed in the remarkable time of three hours and forty minutes. Today, with all the modern appliances of cranes and labour-saving devices, this record is worth noting. Two years later was launched from this yard the famous East Indiaman *Warren Hastings*, which, as will be seen presently, was destined to become famous for her achievement in 1806.

These East Indiamen, the backbone and beauty of the British Marine, were frigate-built, and stately rather than fast sailers, badly designed, requiring much ballast, and essentially but little improved since the sixteenth century. For during the latter part of the eighteenth century it was the French who were the finest naval architects. But two names become associated with the history of this yard before the close of the eighteenth century, and it is with these two families that the golden age of the sailing ship will ever be remembered.

In another chapter we shall see how much the Wigrams and Greens did to make the British ships unique in the annals of sail. It is therefore worth mentioning that in the year 1764 comes the first mention of Robert Wigram. His father had been master of a privateer. After his death the young Robert came to London and was apprenticed to a surgeon. Two years later Wigram took his surgeon's diploma and then sailed in that capacity in one of the East India Company's ships. This was the *Admiral Watson*. Subsequently he also served in the *Duke of Richmond*, but about 1770, after acquiring valuable knowledge of the Eastern trade, he became a merchant, and later one of the proprietors

Brunswick Dock Blackwall

of this yard, his son William afterwards becoming one of the directors of the East India Company. It was in 1782 that George Green was apprenticed to the yard, and owing to his ability and other circumstances, was destined also to become later one of the partners.

It is interesting also to mention that young Wigram, during his voyage in the *Admiral Watson*, formed a friendship with the second officer, whose name was W. T. Money. We thus see the first association of those three names. Money, Wigram and Green, which are inseparable from the finest fleet of sailing ships in its most historic period.

But the time has not arrived to discuss the Victorian ships. The Mercantile Marine of the eighteenth and the first part of the nineteenth century had first to go through most trying times before the blessings of permanent peace should arrive. We who are now alive have not forgotten that for four years during the recent Great War the merchant shipping of the Allies was subject to the attacks of our enemies. But in the past it was for forty years, as we have already seen, the British mercantile vessels had to endure this danger, and it is our duty to observe how our seafaring forefathers carried on during those trying times. The fighting spirit was by no means confined to the Navy, and even apart from those forty years, there hardly seemed a long period when the trading ship could proceed upon her lawful occasions without fear of being attacked. If it was not a pirate, it was a privateer or a warship of some kind. But the merchantman still went about her business all the same, undaunted and undismayed.

We are familiar with ancient works on naval tactics, but there is in the British Museum a rare and somewhat damaged volume, printed in the year 1702, called *The Art of Seafighting*, written by a retired merchant mariner named Robert Park of Ipswich. It was undertaken on behalf of the Merchant Service at a time when the privateers were so active. Park was a "whole-hogger," who knew no difference between foolhardiness and courage. He was a real "hard-case" sailorman, typical of his time, who had no use for luxury, but was a firm believer in trade and liberty. In this volume he tells his readers how to prepare the ship for close-fighting, by making the bulkheads musket-proof, and so on. He tells them how a ship can be worked under fire without showing a man on deck, gives valuable hints on gunnery and the importance of sobriety in the duties of a gunner. In the third part of the book he gives the very same advice which the British Admiralty in the recent war used to issue to the steamship captains. Park sensibly reminds his brother seamen that they are merchantmen, that they are sent to sea not to fight, but to get their cargoes to port, and if possible they are to avoid engagement. Nevertheless it was a wicked crime to leave an attacked consort to become a prey to the enemy.

He gives seamanlike hints on how a three-masted ship should escape. He shows the ship stations and duties when preparing for battle, where the master is to take up his position, where the gunner is to be stationed, what the mate and the carpenter are to be doing. He gives the best tactics with regard to the enemy's boarding, and even discourses on the handling of a fleet of merchantmen, incidentally maintaining that for them the weather-gauge is not usually advantageous. He prefers having a fleet in double, treble or even quadruple line, and gives diagrams. It is a quaint book, of human as well as practical interest, and well indicates the fine spirit of our eighteenth century merchantmen. Those who read it must have found it extraordinarily useful.

It may be as well, before proceeding further, to make quite clear the meaning of the two expressions "privateer" and "Letter of Marque." Legally there was no difference, but in practice a privateer was a vessel which took out a licence for the purpose of cruising against the enemy's merchant ships. In order to send the prizes into port she necessarily carried a large crew. A "Letter of Marque" was a merchant ship with a cargo bound for her port in the usual manner, but possessing this licence which exempted her from convoy, nominally protected her crew from being impressed, and gave her the right to attack an enemy merchantman without having to wait until the latter attacked her. In a word, she was primarily a merchantman, whereas the privateer was a fighting merchant cruiser.

But these British merchant captains were as clever as they were brave. Take the following incident, which occurred at the end of January 1797 off the east end of Java. Here the French Rear-Admiral Sercey, with a squadron of six frigates, was at sea when five homeward-bound British East Indiamen came in sight. These five were all richly laden, and their first duty was certainly to get their cargoes to England and fight only if inevitable. The names of the British ships were the *Woodford, Ocean, Taunton Castle, Canton* and the *Boddam*. These five were in charge of the senior officer, Captain Charles Lennox. The latter took the situation in at once, and realised that it would be useless to run away.

Moreover the mere act of so doing would indicate the inferiority of his squadron; so he did a very smart thing. He hoisted the flag of

Rear-Admiral Rainier at the mizzen, and made the other four ships hoist pendants and ensigns as if they were men-of-war.

Furthermore, in order to maintain this gigantic piece of bluff, he actually detached two of his ships to give chase and reconnoitre the French squadron, and as these daring craft approached the *Cybele*, the latter crowded on sail to join her consorts and made the signal at her masthead: "*L'ennemi est supérieur aux forces Françaises.*" Thereupon the French Admiral also made sail. He certainly thought it curious that when another of his frigates, the *Forte*, carried away her maintopmast the British did not continue the chase, but the captain of *Cybele* hailed him, whilst passing, that he had made out the enemy to consist of two line-of-battle ships and four frigates! Admiral Sercey therefore continued his retreat, and the East Indiamen were never engaged. It was not till a month later that he realised how he had been fooled.

The mere fact that a French naval officer should have taken East Indiamen for line-of-battle ships is at once a proof of the stateliness and formidable appearance which the company's ships possessed. It shows the great similarity which existed at that time between the ships of war and of commerce. But finer even than this exploit was the following brilliant achievement, which is one of the brightest incidents in the whole story of the Merchant Service.

It was on January 31, 1804, that sixteen East Indiamen set forth from Canton for Europe. They were all of a size of from 1200 to 1500 tons register, their names being the *Earl Camden, Warley, Alfred, Royal George, Coutts, Wexford, Ganges, Exeter, Earl of Abergavenny, Henry Addington, Bombay Castle, Cumberland, Hope, Dorsetshire, Warren Hastings*, and *Ocean*. The senior officer present was Captain Nathaniel Dance, in the *Earl Camden*, and so was Commodore of all these ships. But it was a fleet rather than a squadron, for, in addition to the above sixteen, forty more vessels were also put under his charge to convoy them as far as their courses remained the same. A convoy of forty sailing ships! What a magnificent sight they presented, most of them carrying royals and staysails, and the massive hulls with their stern galleries and ornate figure-heads and painted ports heeling over gracefully to the wind!

For Commodore Dance it was a most responsible task. This fleet was carrying many thousand pounds' worth of goods. There was the danger of pirates and the possibility of falling in with the French men-of-war; and there was the ever-present danger of collision. But those were the days of seamanship, and where would you find today any mercantile or naval officer who could handle a fleet of forty sail? We know all too well how difficult it was to handle much smaller convoys of steam-ships during the recent war; and with engines it is mere child's play compared with dependence on wind and sail. To Commodore Dance, then, I suggest the greatest compliment is due for his leadership and tactical seamanship alone. But that was not all.

Through night and day for a fortnight he kept his fleet under way without mishap, and then at daybreak one February day when the fleet was E.N.E. of Pulo-Auro, which was visible, the *Royal George* made a signal that she had sighted four strange sail to the south-west. Commodore Dance therefore signalled the *Alfred, Royal George, Bombay Castle* and *Hope* to go down and examine them. It happened that in the Commodore's ship there was a passenger named Lieutenant Robert Fowler, R.N., lately in command of a ship that had been wrecked. He now offered to go in the fast-sailing brig *Ganges*, which was in the convoy. The Commodore assented, and she went away also to examine the strange vessels. Before long the look-out ships signalled that the strangers were actually a French squadron consisting of a line-of-battle ship, three frigates and a brig.

At 1 p.m. the British Commodore signalled his scouts to return, and formed the line of battle in close order. Admiral Linois, who was in command of the French squadron, as soon as he could fetch in the wake of the East Indiamen, put about. The Commodore expected his rear to be attacked, but at nightfall the enemy, preferring a daylight action, hauled close to the wind. The British ships lay-to all night, the men at their quarters, ready for action, and at daybreak the enemy were seen also lying-to, but were three miles to windward. Both forces now hoisted their colours, and as the whole of the China fleet had been only recently painted, they presented a wonderful sight with their clouds of canvas. Admiral Linois' flag was in the 74-gun ship *Marengo*, his other units being the 40-gun frigate *Belle-Poule*, the 36-gun frigate *Sémillante*, the 22-gun *Berceau*, and the 16-gun *Aventurier*. It was no chance meeting, for the French Admiral was on the lookout for this China fleet, of whose strength and time of departure he had been informed.

At 9 a.m., as the enemy showed no intention of engaging, Dance formed the order of sailing and continued his course, his fleet being under easy sail on the starboard tack; whereupon the French filled and edged towards the merchantmen. Four hours later, as it was obvious that Linois was trying to cut off the rear of the fleet. Dance signalled his fleet to tack in succession, bear down in line ahead, and engage on

CAPTAIN HENRY WILSON,
A commanding officer in the H.E. India
Company, who was wrecked in the com-
pany's ship "Antelope." About 1788.

CAPTAIN HON. RICHARD WALPOLE,
Who commanded the H.E. India Company's
ship "New Houghton." About 1805.

COMMODORE SIR NATHANIEL DANCE,
1804.
A very gallant mercantile officer.

SIR WILLIAM JAMES, BART.,
Commodore in the H.E. India Company,
Chairman of the Court of Directors, etc.
About 1805.

FOUR PORTRAITS WILSON, WALPOLE, DANSE AND BART

arriving abreast of the enemy. This manoeuvre was perfectly carried out, the *Royal George* leading, all of them in close order and under t'gallant sails.[1] At 1.15 p.m. Linois opened fire upon the *Royal George* and leading ships, but this was returned in a very determined manner. For about three-quarters of an hour the two enemies blazed away at each other. The brunt was borne by the *Royal George*, but the *Ganges, Earl Camden, Warley* and *Alfred* were all hotly engaged. These five ships gave the French such a hot time that by two o'clock *Marengo* and her consorts ceased firing, hauled their wind, broke off the engagement and stood away under all sail to the eastward. The French warships had been beaten by British merchantmen and especially by clever tactics. But that was not all.

Dance now made the signal for a general chase, and for two hours these merchant ships chased the warships; and then, remembering that his first duty was to his ships and their valuable cargoes. Dance feared that further pursuit would take his fleet too far from the mouth of the Malacca Straits, so ordered his fleet to tack, and eventually entered the straits. The *Royal George* had one man killed, one wounded, and she received some shot holes in her hull and sails; the other British ships were practically untouched. The sixteen East Indiamen carried from thirty to thirty-six guns each, though not one of these ships was armed better than the *Aventurier*, and this point is to be remembered, that a warship is always more or less ready to fight, whereas these East Indiamen were full of cargo and the decks were greatly lumbered.

The Commodore by his determination and promptitude had saved the whole fleet, and it is to the credit of these sixteen merchantmen that their smart appearance, the regularity of their manoeuvres, and their bold advance made the French Admiral wonder whether, after all, these were not British men-of-war escorting the others. For this remarkable victory the Commodore, officers and crews were liberally rewarded. The Patriotic Fund Committee, which had originated m Lloyd's coffee-house in 1803, presented the Commodore with a sword of the value of £100 and a silver vase of the same worth.

Captain Timmins of the *Royal George* also received a sword, as did the other captains and Lieutenant Fowler. The directors of the East India Company set aside about £50,000, and rewarded their Commodore with 2000 guineas and a piece of plate valued at 200 guineas. Captain Timmins received 1000 guineas and plate, the other captains receiving 500 guineas each and a piece of plate. The chief officers

1 For list of an East Indiaman's sails, see Appendix. 100

each received 150 guineas, the second officers 125 guineas, and so on through the ship, each seaman receiving six guineas.

Dance was given also £5000 by the Bombay Insurance Society. He was offered a baronetcy, but declined it and accepted a knighthood, and thus concludes one of the finest incidents in the history of the Merchant Service. This action showed that the ships and men were not merely magnificent for their own particular job, but that they could tackle any emergency that came along.

CHAPTER 10

Mighty Merchantmen

Most of the vessels in this fleet of East Indiamen had been built at the Blackwall yard, or at least refitted there. In the year 1789 the East India Docks were brought into being, or rather begun, for they were not opened for another couple of years. This wet dock had become very necessary, for the East Indiamen had no accommodation provided for them now that they had become so big. And as long as they lay out in the river a good deal of their valuable cargoes was subject to pilfering. A joint-stock company was formed with a capital of £200,000, and it was decided that the hatches of every ship arriving from either India or China should be locked down before the ship reached Gravesend, and that the captain and one officer should remain on board until the ship was moored in the docks and the keys of the hatches handed over to an officer of the East India Company.

At the beginning of the nineteenth century the price of building these ships was £13 12s. 6d. a ton. By 1803 it had gone up to £19. Five years later there were ten of these ships lost; in fact the first decade of the new century was unfortunate generally. There were losses owing to disasters at sea, and the French war paralysed the Indian trade. But the Blackwall yard was kept busy, and in 1813 it built ten frigates for the British Government of from 1078 to 1571 tons, owing to the lessons which had been learnt from the American frigates. Having built so many East Indiamen, this mercantile yard was eminently fitted for constructing such craft. And now that the firm consisted of Sir Robert Wigram, George Green, Money Wigram and Henry Loftus Wigram, we can see the time approaching when the famous Blackwall frigates were to make their appearance, though we shall not come to them immediately.

In 1814 was launched for the East India Company the 1263-ton

Lady Melville, and the firm of Wigrams & Greens was now making a great deal of money. Three years later came the fine 1325-ton *Waterloo*. The only other port in the kingdom that in any way rivalled London was Liverpool. In 1751 there were only 220 ships belonging to Liverpool, but the opening of the American trade five years later gave it a great impetus. Then came those years of war which checked this, but on the resumption of peace in 1815 the Mercantile Marine received a wonderful impetus which has culminated in the magnificent Atlantic liners of today. There was the great industrial awakening in Yorkshire and Lancashire, a big trade was to be built up with America, and the haven of the Mersey was geographically suitable for the exports and imports. Britain was supreme at sea, foreign shipping had almost disappeared, the demand for tonnage was increasing rapidly, and the Mercantile Marine was very much encouraged. In fact, from 1815 to 1860 the service passed through the most popular days of its long career.

The first thirty years of the nineteenth century, just before the Indian monopoly was lost, saw the East India Company ships at their very best. We have spoken of the "Merchant Service" as a generic term, for convenience; but, strictly speaking, it pertained to the service in the ships of the East India Company, to distinguish it from service in the Free Traders and the Royal Navy. During this time to be able to get into the company's service was about as good as a commission in the navy. The ships themselves were as fine as any naval corvette, with similar discipline and similar personnel. Run like men-of-war, owned by a very ancient and wealthy company of unique' character, the officers were of a social status equal to their cousins and brothers in His Majesty's vessels. It was only when this old monopoly was taken away, and the romantic mixture of trade and sea-adventure gave way to keen competition in the race for wealth, that ships, officers, men and methods became of a different standard for a time. But this is always excepting the famous Blackwall frigates, which were destined to keep up the fine traditions of the old Indiamen.

An officer in the East India Company was made to realise that he was being honoured to be allowed to enter such a service. The captains and first four officers were always sworn in before being allowed to proceed to duty on board. They enjoyed the very lucrative privilege of being able to participate in the company's monopoly. The captain of a 755-ton ship and upwards, for instance, was allowed as much as fifty-six tons for his private trade, and he could even do better than this by using as dunnage bamboos which could be sold in London. From China he could bring home 9336 lbs. Therefore, although his pay was only £10 a month—and we must not forget that a sovereign in those days was worth very much more than it is today—the captain was able to make very nice profits. The officers were also allowed a liberal amount of wine, beer, butter, cheese, spirits and groceries. No wonder that an officer was so often able to retire after a very few voyages and buy a ship for himself.

The 1200-ton *East Indiaman* carried a captain, six mates, surgeon, purser, boatswain-gunner, master-at-arms, midshipmen, caulker, cooper, cooks, carpenters, quartermasters, sailmaker, armourer, butcher, baker, poulterer, officers' servants, stewards; the crew numbering a hundred and thirty. No one could become captain unless he had voyaged to and from India or China as chief or second mate. These officers were better seamen than navigators, but navigation was still crude and somewhat unscientific in those days. The full uniform of the captain was a fine blue coat with black Genoa velvet round the cuffs, black velvet lapels, black velvet panteen cape. The gilt buttons bore the company's crest. Whenever officers appeared before the Court of Directors they were compelled to wear full uniform, but undress uniform when appearing before the Committee.

Strict instructions were given to the captain that his new hands were to wear the clothes provided by the company. The pay of the "forcmast men" was £2 5s. a month, but in addition to this they were entitled to a pension from what was known as the Poplar Fund. Any captain, officer or man who had served aboard these ships for eight years and had regularly contributed to the fund was entitled to a pension. The size of the pension was based on the amount of capital which an officer possessed. Thus, if a captain said he was not worth £2500, or £125 a year, he received a pension of £100. Allowances were made to the widows and orphans of those who had served the company for seven years, and if a man had been wounded or maimed so as to be incapable of further sea service he was qualified for a pension even if he had not served eight years.

We mentioned some time back the fine East Indiaman *Warren Hastings*. In the engagement which is to be described she lost her purser and six men, and thirteen were wounded, including her chief, third and sixth officers and surgeon's mate. Therefore, although these were really merchant ships, built to carry cargoes, with neither the facilities nor the crew of a man-of-war, yet there was always the possibility of the personnel being killed or disabled for life. In the case of the *Warren Hastings*, extra special trouble had been taken to enable her to defend herself against any French frigate she might meet. She mounted twenty-six 18-pounders on her main or lower deck, fourteen on her upper deck, and four 12-pounders on her poop. She left England in February 1805 and reached China, then left again for home, but in a less suitable condition of defence; for of her main-deck ports four had been caulked up so as to give space for a storeroom, and the four guns had been placed in the hold. Of her crew, forty Chinamen remained at Canton, and a British man-of-war had pressed eighteen of her English seamen. Four of her upper-deck guns had also been stowed below. She therefore now mounted only thirty-six guns.

It was on June 21 at 7.30 a.m., when the ship was in Lat. 26° 13' S., Long. 56° 45' E. that *Warren Hastings*, steering W. by S. before a strong breeze from N.E. by E., under a press of sail, sighted to the southwest a strange ship under treble-reefed topsails and courses. This was the French 40-gun frigate *Piémontaise*, 1093 tons, with a crew of 385, and able to fire a broadside of twenty-three guns, against the *Warren Hastings'* eighteen. The latter had a tonnage of 1356, but a crew of only 138. The Frenchman had twenty-eight 18-pounders on her main deck. She also carried eighteen other guns on her quarter-deck, a total of forty-six carriage-guns. But she also carried swivels and musketoons in her tops and along her gunwales.

On each fore and main yard-arm there was a tripod to contain a 5-cwt. shell, so that if she got alongside her enemy its fusee could be lit by a man lying out on the yard, and it would then be allowed to fall on the enemy's deck, and after its explosion the French would be able to rush on board. It was thus in idea a revival of mediævalism. The historian James even went so far as to refer to the Frenchmen as being "armed more like assassins than men-of-war's men; each having, beside the usual boarding weapons, a poniard struck through the button-holes of his jacket."

Thus, in every respect except tonnage the East Indiaman was a more powerful vessel, and the preliminary tactics are interesting. At 9 a.m., when the Indiaman was well on her weather-quarter, the Frenchman shook out the reefs from her topsails and stood towards the merchantman, who held on her course. Half an hour later the frigate set her t'gallant sails and stuns'ls, and at 10 a.m. hoisted the British blue ensign and pendant. There was nothing wrong in this *ruse de guerre*, and often during the war of 1914-1918 British ships hoisted neutral colours before opening fire on German submarines. *Warren Hastings* suspected the frigate was not a British man-of-war, but hoisted her colours and made her private signal. For, in order that East Indiamen might be able to make themselves known on the high seas to British men-of-war, a special code of signals was always arranged by the Admiralty during war-time. This code was sent sealed to the Secret Committee of the company and then handed over to the commanding officer of each ship.

The Frenchman took no notice of the signals, continued rapidly to approach, so that at 11 a.m. the Indiaman shortened sail and cleared for action: it was quite obvious now what was going to happen. At noon the frigate took in her stuns'ls, staysails and mainsail, and then hauled down British colours and hoisted French. After opening fire and disabling part of the Indiaman's rigging, the Frenchman again attacked, this time killing and wounding several of the merchantman's crew, badly damaging the foremast, cutting away all the foreshrouds on the port side and the ensign. The latter was quickly hoisted again at the maintopgallant masthead.

A third attack followed, during which the *Warren Hastings'* foremast was finally crippled. Thus, owing to the wind and heavy sea, the latter could carry sail on only her main and mizzen masts, and now opened fire. A hot engagement followed, and unfortunately her mainmast was now damaged as well as her standing and running rigging, besides the further loss of men killed and wounded. The fifth attack found her with only the main topsail set, and the enemy poured in a terrible fire, which knocked the spanker boom into splinters and carried away the mizzen mast, which, falling forward, disabled every remaining effective gun on the upper deck.

Troubles came not singly, for the lower deck was on fire, the rudder was rendered useless, and whilst the surgeon was operating, a shell entered and destroyed all his instruments. For four hours and a half the Indiaman had sought to defend herself, but in spite of the zeal and perseverance of her officers and men she was compelled in her crippled state to lower her colours. Then, being thoroughly unmanageable, the Indiaman, with the heavy sea running, happened to fall off, and crashed alongside the *Piémontaise*, who was to leeward. Thereupon a number of Frenchmen leapt aboard the merchantman with daggers and threatened to kill the lot, dragged the captain about the ship and accused him of having tried to ram the frigate so as to cripple her masts; and then stabbed the captain, whereupon he fainted through loss of blood. The second officer, surgeon, and a midshipman and boatswain's mate were similarly stabbed. Presently this fury died down, the Frenchman took the Englishman in tow and both arrived at the Isle of France on July 4.

Thus, life in these merchant ships, although well rewarded, was at any time during those long years of hostilities liable suddenly to become most exciting. Ships and men were sent to the bottom or taken captive, but the service went on. Lest the reader should imagine these incidents isolated events, let the following be related. On May 2, 1809, a small squadron of homeward-bound Indiamen had cleared the Sandheads of Bengal River, escorted by H.M. sloop *Victor*. After three weeks the latter, in dark and squally weather of the night of the 24th, parted company. By the 30th, owing to stress of weather, two ships had left the convoy, and there now remained only the *Streatham, Europe* and *Lord Keith* in company. The first two were 820-ton craft; the third was a vessel of 600 tons. The first two carried thirty guns apiece; the *Lord Keith* had not more than twelve.

At five-thirty on the morning of May 31, when in Lat. 9° 15' N., Long. 90° 30' E., these three were on the starboard tack with the wind S.W. by S. when a strange ship was seen seven miles off to the west of south. This was the French 40-gun frigate *Caroline*, which mounted forty-six guns in addition to her swivels. She had been cruising off the Sandheads and had captured a few ships. Subsequently she had learned from an American ship, the *Silenus*, which had sailed from the Sandheads, of the number and probable route of the Indiamen. But when first sighted the *Caroline* was taken by the Indiamen for the *Victor. Streatham*, being the senior ship, made the private signal about 6 a.m., but having got no answer from the Frenchman, signalled the other two to form into line. *Lord Keith* leading, followed by *Streatham* and *Europe*, but the two last mentioned were a considerable distance apart.

Half an hour later the *Caroline* hoisted colours and attacked *Europe*, who quickly returned the fire. At the end of half an hour the latter was disabled. Most of her guns were put out of action, yards, foremast, sails and rigging cut to pieces and hull damaged in several places. And then the enemy raked her from forward and proceeded to deal with *Streatham*, which by eight o'clock was so utterly crippled that she had to lower colours. Meanwhile *Lord Keith* and *Europe* had been firing at *Caroline*, who now recommenced the action with the last mentioned. Presently *Europe* closed *Streatham*, but on learning that the latter had surrendered, and that *Lord Keith* had escaped, running before the wind, also determined to up helm. Then *Caroline*, after securing *Streatham*, went in chase and captured *Europe*.

On account of the leaking condition which the two prizes were now in, it took three days to get them in a sea-worthy condition, but on July 22, with their valuable cargoes, they were brought by *Caroline* and anchored in the Bay of St. Paul, Isle of Bourbon. It had been a heavy loss to the East India Company, though the gallant merchant captains, with their ill-armed and badly-manned ships (the crews consisting partly of cowardly Portuguese and lascars), had done all that was possible. The one consoling feature was that *Lord Keith* managed to get right away, and actually arrived safely back in English waters.

Similarly on July 8, 1810, three outward-bound Indiamen, the *Ceylon, Windham* and *Astell*, each of them of 800 tons, were about thirty miles west of the island of Mayotta on a northerly course with a fresh S.S.E. breeze when three ships were sighted close-hauled on the port tack. These were the two French frigates *Bellone, Minerve*, and the recaptured ship-corvette *Victor*, about nine miles distant, and it was about six o'clock, just as the day was dawning. Half an hour later the senior Indiaman *Ceylon* made the private signal, and, as no answer was returned, the merchant ships prepared for action. Presently, as *Astell* signalled she was overpressed, the other two shortened sail. Captain Meriton made the following signal from *Ceylon*: "As we cannot get away, I think we had better go under easy sail, and bring them to action before dark."

To this *Astell* replied: " Certainly."

Windham answered: "If we make all sail and get into smooth water under the land, we can engage to more advantage."

The wind increased so much that the Indiamen were compelled to heave-to, and took in the third reef of their topsails. It was not an ideal day for an engagement, as the ships heeled over so that they could not keep open their lower-deck ports. Captain Meriton formed his ships in line abreast, *Ceylon* in the centre, and at 2.15 p.m. *Minerve* opened fire on *Windham* and *Ceylon*. There was a heavy sea running and the action became general. During the afternoon Captain Hay of *Astell* was severely wounded, and the command was taken over by the chief mate. *Windham* had her sails and rigging considerably damaged, and about 4.30 p.m. a temporary lull occurred, when *Minerve* carried away her main and mizzen topmasts. And then Captain Meriton was wounded, so the command of *Ceylon* devolved on her chief mate,

PICTURE OF CONVOY OF EAST INDIAMEN

who a few minutes afterwards was himself wounded and was succeeded by the second mate.

This ship had received great punishment throughout the engagement: her masts, sails and rigging were badly damaged, many of her guns disabled, her hull so injured that she was making three feet of water an hour; six of her people were killed and twenty-one wounded. Therefore before half-past seven she hauled down her colours and was taken prize. *Astell*, already much injured, put out her lights, made sail and escaped during the extreme darkness of the night. *Windham* was now left alone, and finding that she was too damaged to make sail, continued the action to help *Astell's* escape, and then hauled down her colours and was taken captive.

The captains, officers and men had fought very gallantly against the French, who were in superior force, and the East India Company, who always could afford to treat their servants handsomely, awarded each of the three captains the sum of £500, with a fine reward for the officers and men. On Captain Hay of the *Astell* the company also settled a pension of £460 a year, and distributed £2000 among the officers and crew. Furthermore, the Admiralty, to show their appreciation of the ship's gallantry, granted to the crew a protection from impressment for three years. One of the men, Andrew Peters, had bravely nailed the pendant to the maintop masthead, and having done so was killed while descending the rigging.

It is fine to read of the resource, the able seamanship and great gallantry of these wonderful old ships right through two centuries until well into a third. But there was a new era coming, and the final link with Tudor romance and mediaeval shipping ideas was just about to be severed. Looking back on events, it seems to us moderns perfectly amazing that the East India Company should have enjoyed so rich and enormous a monopoly so long, and in the year 1814 they lost this privilege so far as India was concerned. The result was that a new impetus was given to ship-building and ship-owning, and the element of competition was introduced with free trade and no favour.

In the task of making the Mercantile Marine of Britain such a solid, dignified, stately and honourable service for all those years the company did much; nor is this influence by any means dead, for it set a high standard for subsequent independent ship-owners to follow, and it permeates the big shipping lines of today. What the Orient had meant in a small way to the Tudor and Stuart seamen and merchants, it was to mean on a much bigger scale to the traders of the nineteenth century, and the wealth of Great Britain was to benefit thereby.

From 1814 the owners of the Blackwall yard began to build East Indiamen for themselves to own and manage. In 1824 they built the *Carn Brae Castle*, 570 tons, which was the first ship expressly built for the passenger trade to Calcutta, and the finest ship of her day. She was lost rather unnecessarily by the officer of the watch allowing her to stand too close into Freshwater Bay, Isle of Wight, one day when the captain and passengers were at dinner.

In that same year Mr. Green had purchased the *Sir Edward Paget*, which was the first of the well-known passenger ships to India and Australia. She was elaborately fitted and made quite a sensation. She was commanded by Captain Geary, R.N., and in this connection the following true anecdote is recorded. The house flag which she wore was a white ground with a red St. George's cross through the centre. One day, after arrival at Spithead, the Admiral at Portsmouth sent his lieutenant off to inquire what ship was wearing an admiral's flag, and on learning that she was a merchant ship, at once ordered it to be hauled down. A blue handkerchief was then sown on the centre of the flag, and as this satisfied the lieutenant it was allowed to be hoisted again, and continued to be the distinguishing flag of the Wigram and Green ships until, some years later, the partnership in the firm was dissolved.

After this ship returned to Blackwall from her first voyage, Mr. Green proceeded on board to make his usual inspection, and, much to his dismay, was received with manned yards, with a salute, and the ship's band playing "The Conquering Hero." But the *Sir Edward Paget* was not a man-of-war and Mr. Green was not an admiral; and it was all very fine, but not suitable. He resented this kind of reception, and the general man-of-war appearance everywhere on board so astonished him, that he was not surprised also to find that when the accounts of the voyage were balanced the style was not financially profitable. The result was that a new captain came to the ship and there was a new set of regulations before she went on her second voyage.

In 1825 a couple of 1325-ton ships were launched by the yard, and here we get the final resemblance to the ships of the *Caroline* period, for the figurehead, poop, decorations and so on have been considerably modified. By the year 1830 the firm had ceased to build any more vessels to be employed by the East India Company; for although that corporation had lost its Indian monopoly, as already stated, it still retained a like privilege in regard to China. But the public mind was opposed to this being continued; in 1832 Parliament had to face the question, and in April of 1834 the company lost its commercial charter forever. But, seeing this revolution was approaching, individual firms had in the meantime been preparing to compete in this Eastern trade. Not merely did the Greens and Wigrams from 1830 build ships for themselves, but they ordered them from the Tyne firm of T. & W. Smith, and this firm also began to own East Indiamen themselves in competition with the Greens and Wigrams.

In 1831 the Blackwall firm consisted of George Green, Money Wigram, Henry Loftus Wigram, Richard Green and Henry Green, but they were to pursue a strange policy, which, if good for the Mercantile Marine, was destined to ruin the firm. The owners of the Blackwall yard began to build ships not for the firm, but for individual members of the firm—so many for the Green family and so many for the Wigrams, but especially for the former. Thus it came about that a Green fleet competed with a Wigram fleet, whilst by the year 1841 the ships owned by the firm itself numbered only two. Finally in 1843 the partnership was dissolved.

But in 1832 they launched the 577-ton *London* for Money Wigram, and this was the real pioneer of the celebrated Blackwall frigates of which we shall speak in a later chapter. We thus enter on that last stage of ship development which was to precede the golden age of the sailing ship, when the clippers made eternal fame for themselves. This yard was still the biggest private concern in Europe, though Liverpool as a great port was now going ahead. The beginning of the American War in 1812 had given it a serious set-back, but after peace came in 1814 there was a new era as well for the Atlantic shipping as for the East. For America was going ahead. She had shown that she knew how to build during the war frigates of an improved kind, and in peace she was now producing better designed merchantmen than ourselves.

In 1816 was inaugurated the famous Black Ball Line of New York packets, which were the precursors of the present-day Atlantic liners. These Black Ball liners were full-rigged ships of from 300 to 500 tons register, with full bodies and bluff bows, and yet they averaged at first only twenty-three days on the outward voyage to Liverpool and forty-three days homeward-bound. This was the only means of communication in those days between America and Liverpool, and in 1836 was started the Dramatic Line, consisting of 700-ton sailing ships. The world's trade was increasing, industrialism was prospering, the markets of the whole world were now open to all, and there was a long spell of peace ahead. Transatlantic shipping was encouraged so that these packet ships increased in tonnage, and in 1846 the 1400-ton *New World* was built, being then the largest sailing ship in the world. Other famous vessels were the *Isaac Webb, Albert Webb* and *Guy Mannering*. The ships of these two lines were exceedingly fine craft, and made remarkable passages across to England, the Black Ball liners eventually averaging twenty-one days and the Dramatic liners twenty and a half days. The nineteenth century in regard to the sailing ship alone was certainly a most wonderful period.

Picture of a fine piece of seamanship

CHAPTER 11

Packet Ships and Brigs

As far back as the reign of Elizabeth a State post-office was instituted for foreign letters, for the reason that the merchants now required
it. Owing to England's geographical position, this, of course, connot-
ed the employment of sailing ships. By 1635 the weekly continental
service was doubled and accelerated. This arrangement improved during the seventeenth century, and there were packet stations at Dover
for France, Harwich and Yarmouth for Holland and Hamburg, and at
Holyhead and Milford for Ireland.

But it was Falmouth which became the head-quarters for the post-
office packet service as far back as 1688. The reason for this is obvious
when you consider its location in regard to the Bay of Biscay, and the
facility with which even those unhandy sailing craft could come in
and out in all weathers and practically all winds. A very safe harbour,
with plenty of room and water, right at the western end of the English
Channel and easy of access, it was ideal for the departure of travellers
and mails for Spain and the West Indies. The result was that, as the
service became more numerous, shipyards were created in Falmouth,
inns were built for the travellers, and a seafaring population grew up.

The North Sea packets were of about sixty tons, but the Falmouth
packets were of 200 tons and heavily armed. They were not owned
by the post-office, but hired by private contract, as the East India
Company used to charter their ships. In fact, never did the post-office
own the ships, although the officers and men were its servants, and
not the contractor's. The Falmouth packet service began in a quiet
way in 1688 with the hiring of two craft, and for years it was run at a
loss. But there were political reasons for keeping up connection with
Spain, and during the eighteenth century both the Spanish and West
Indian trades became important; and even by 1702 packet ships from

Falmouth were running to Barbados, Jamaica, the southern States of North America, to Corunna in Spain, and in 1704 also to Lisbon.

It was a separate method of causing to grow up a body of fine seamen; it was one of the best schools for encouraging navigation, which was still in a most crude position; and generally it was one of the great influences towards building up the Mercantile Marine. It was not until Cromwell's time that any real naval fighting service as distinct from the Merchant Navy had come into being, and right up to the Napoleonic Wars the two services were closely allied and practically interchangeable. We have to remember also that merchantmen and packet ships had to fight enemy warships whenever required. Of a peaceful voyage there was hardly such a thing.

Such incidents as that of May 16, 1744, when the *Townshend* packet fought against the Spaniards; or of July 25, 1759, when the packet *Fawkener* was attacked by a large French sloop between Barbados and Antigua, are by no means isolated. Indeed, although they were forbidden to seek engagements and were reminded that their first duty was the safety of the mails, yet if they saw a chance of obtaining wealth at sea by attacking a likely ship, they did so in spite of any authority. These men were, like the age in which they lived, a hardy, rough, corrupt lot of dare-devils.

They carried cargoes of their own, contrary to regulations; they stole, they smuggled, they mutinied—but we cannot go through the whole decalogue. On the other hand, they were real sailormen, and the rule that a packet was to put to sea from Falmouth immediately on receiving the mails, whatever the wind might be, provided only she could carry a double-reefed topsail, was maintained. The regularity of their voyages was the nearest thing to the running of a modern steamship.

In 1798 there were sixteen packet ships to keep up the Falmouth to West Indies service, and "on the quiet" captains, officers and crews would take out quantities of cheese, potatoes, boots, shoes and so on, sell them on commission for English merchants, and then bring back such goods as wines, lace, tobacco, brandy, which would be smuggled ashore and then sold all over the country by special men. This went on until 1810, when the Lisbon and West Indian packets were strictly forbidden to carry on these trades. The order brought the crews up with a round turn, and a terrible moan went about in disgust. Their wages were certainly too low, and this was the means of remunerating themselves. Anger and indignation finally culminated in a mutiny.

And yet the captains used to make no meagre living, even reckoned in the money of the nineteenth century. They were paid £8 a month during war-time and £5 in peace; but besides this they received large sums in respect of the fares of passengers. One captain alone was making £1000 a year by this means, and then there were the fees for carrying bullion, to say nothing of their commission for selling goods, both exports and imports. For instance, they were paid thirty-five guineas by every passenger who proceeded from Falmouth to Gibraltar. By the year 1808 there were thirty-nine packets at Falmouth—quite a fine fleet for any one port in those days.

Every week one sailed for Lisbon, one for San Sebastian or other part of the north Spanish coast, whence communication with the British army in the Peninsula was maintained. Each week, too, one packet sailed for the West Indies, whilst others at longer intervals set forth towards the Mediterranean, Brazil, Surinam, Halifax and New York. People were beginning to travel, and between 2000 and 3000 passengers thus passed through Falmouth to and from these ships yearly. It was a very encouraging factor for the Mercantile Marine, especially as the Falmouth packets alone kept 1200 men permanently employed afloat.

Contemporary artists of the early nineteenth century have left for us paintings showing some of the North Sea packet ships. Turner's well-known picture in the National Gallery of the English packet arriving in Calais in 1803 is an instance. These craft were never bigger than about eighty tons, and during the French wars ran for a time between Yarmouth and Helvoetsluis in Holland. But a West Indian packet such as the Duke of Marlborough with her 1804 tons and brig-rigged, was a very different sort of ship. And in the very year when Commodore Dance put Admiral Linois to flight, this packet ship, whilst bound for the Leeward Islands, was in the month of April chased by a schooner and captured.

As mentioned in the last chapter, the famous American packets which ran from New York to Liverpool, came out in 1816. This famous Black Ball Line was for years the pioneer, and began with five 400-ton ships. During the first ten years these vessels averaged twenty-three days on the eastward and forty-three days on the westward voyage, the fastest eastward being the passage of *Canada* in fifteen days eighteen hours. These ships were flush-decked. Between the foremast and mainmast was the galley, and in the long-boat were carried the sheep and pigs and fowls for the ship's food. A cow was also carried in

CAPTAIN ROGERS

CAPTAIN HUDDART

a house over the main hatch, and the passengers' cabins were aft.

These liners carried a black ball painted on the foresail and were commanded by real hard-case captains who had caused much anxiety to British shipping whilst in command of privateers during the war of 1812. In these ships passengers, mails and bullion were conveyed, two vessels leaving each month. In 1821 two more lines were started, one of which was the Red Star Line of packets to Liverpool. After the Dramatic Line was founded in 1836 the packet ships gradually increased to about 1000 tons, and the competition had become keener, packets now running from North America to Liverpool, Havre and London. Captain A. H. Clark, in his interesting volume *The Clipper Ship Era,* states that all packet ships carried a white light at the bowsprit cap from sunset to sunrise; but of course side-lights had not yet come in.

It is interesting to remark in this connection that probably the first institution of side-lights was in 1834, for from January 1 the City of Dublin Steam Company began to use a white light at the foremast head, a red on the larboard bow and a white on the starboard bow, the two latter being attached to the houses forward of the paddleboxes. Then for a few years there was a diversity in practice, each company doing what it thought best in this respect to minimise risk of collision at sea.

Up to 1846 the system in use by the British packet ships of Liverpool was to have a white light under the cross-trees below the foot of the foresail, with a red light on the port paddlebox and a white light on the starboard paddlebox, but apparently the Milford steam packets carried a red light on the starboard bow, a green light on the port bow and a "common light" (presumably white) at the foremast head. It is claimed that this was also the fashion adopted by the P. & O. Company. In 1846 the Royal Mail Steam Company's ships carried masthead and bow lights, but colourless. The subject is a little difficult to elucidate, but it is certain that there were in existence different usages as late as this date, and it was not until at least two years later that any sort of uniformity came in. It has been stated by another authority that it was only as a result of the collision between the Collins liner *Arctic* and the French ship *Vesta* on September 21, 1854, when the former foundered with the loss of 323 lives out of 368, that the carrying of side-lights was made compulsory and not optional.

Even in the American packets most of the crew were British, and often enough gaol-birds of the worst type, but the captains were pretty tough and accustomed to handling men as well as ships, and the mates were of the same order. These ships could reel off their twelve knots pretty regularly, and sometimes did the voyage in sixteen days. With their high-steeved bowsprits, their black hulls and square painted ports, and carrying plenty of canvas, even to sky sails and stun'sls in summer weather, they used to race against each other, sometimes even for very high stakes. For quite a long time the Atlantic packet ships were able to laugh at the steamships, but gradually from 1840 the progress of the marine engineer and shipbuilder wore down the competition. Regularity and reliability of running with increased comfort were bound to have their influence on the carrying of mails, passengers and merchandise.

Ralph Waldo Emerson in his *English Traits* has left on record an account of his passage across the Atlantic from Boston in 1847 aboard the packet ship *Washington Irving*. She was of 750 tons register, the mainmast measured 115 feet from deck to truck, and the length of the ship from stem to stern on deck was 155 feet.

"The shortest sea-line," he goes on to remark, "from Boston to Liverpool is 2850 miles. This a steamer keeps, saving 150 miles. A sailing ship can never go in a shorter line than 3000, and usually it is much longer. Our good master keeps his kites up to the last moment, studding sails alow and aloft, and by incessant straight steering never loses a rod of way.... Since the ship was built, it seems, the master never slept but in his day-clothes whilst on board.... Hour for hour, the risk on a steamboat is greater; but the speed is safety, or twelve days of danger instead of twenty-four."

In one week the *Washington Irving* made 1467 miles, but to Emerson, as to most passengers in those days, this form of travel was anything but pleasant.

"I find the sea-life an acquired taste," he sums up rather sadly, "like that for tomatoes and olives. The confinement, cold, motion, noise and odour are not to be dispensed with. The floor of your room is sloped at an angle of twenty or thirty degrees, and I waked every morning with the belief that someone was tipping up my berth. Nobody likes being treated ignominiously, upset, shoved against the side of the house, rolled over, suffocated with bilge, mephitis and stewing oil. We get used to these annoyances at last, but the dread of the sea remains longer. ... Such discomfort and such danger as the narratives of the captain and mate disclose are bad enough as the costly fee we pay for entrance to Europe; but the wonder is always new that any sane man can be a sailor."

Emerson found the worst inconvenience was the lack of light in the cabin, but the fifteen days from the time they left soundings were to him long, joyless and severe.

The American poet James Russell Lowell has left us a character sketch of a chief mate whom he describes as

. . . . not an American, but I should never have guessed it by his speech, which was the purest Cape Cod, and I reckon myself a good taster of dialects. . . . He used to walk the deck with his hands in his pockets, in seeming abstraction, but nothing escaped his eye. . . . He is as impervious to cold as the polar bear. On the Atlantic, if the wind blew a gale from the north-east, and it was cold as an English summer, he was sure to turn out in a calico shirt and trousers, his furzy brown chest half bare, and slippers without stockings.

But . . . he comes out in a monstrous pea-jacket here in the Mediterranean when the evening is so hot that Adam would have been glad to leave off his fig-leaves. . . . He . . . always combs his hair, and works himself into a black frock-coat (on Sundays he adds a waistcoat) before he comes to meals, sacrificing himself nobly and painfully to the social proprieties. The second mate, on the other hand, who eats after us, enjoys the privilege of shirt-sleeves, and is, I think, the happier man of the two.

But besides the shipping engaged in the East Indian, West Indian, American, Spanish, Mediterranean and North Sea routes, the Mercantile Marine was being built up by the fishermen and coasters, and we should be providing an inaccurate picture if we did not consider them. In an earlier chapter we saw how important were the fishing fleets down to the end of the seventeenth century, and what a back bone they have always been to the navies and Mercantile Marine. In 1704 Queen Anne reorganised the various laws relating to the herring fishery and permitted the use of all harbours and shores for landing fish on payment of reasonable dues. A certain number of foreigners were being employed by the British to help with the fishing, but in 1747 the Dutch still had 3000 herring vessels and were employing 40,000 fishermen. This was a great falling off since 1679, but still it was a considerable industry, and bringing in £5,000,000. Not without reason these Hollanders called their herring fisheries their gold mine, and in the mid-eighteenth century they were employing over 1000 Englishmen in their craft. Thus each nation learned a good deal of each other's methods, and this standardisation has continued to this day.

Somehow the English fishery companies continued to be unsuccessful, for in October of 1750 one more was incorporated, but the craft and gear were purchased at expensive rates, more fish were obtained than could be sold, and thus the company failed. But it was not merely the Dutch who were rivalling the English and Scottish fishermen. During the latter half of the century the Swedes and the Danes were very active. In fact, British men-of-war had to be requested to afford protection against the encroachments of foreigners. The British fishing craft were often badly built, of ill design and not well found, but legislation was introduced to assist them. In 1771 a bounty of thirty shillings a ton for seven years was granted to all decked vessels of from twenty to eighty tons, provided they were of British origin and ownership and engaged in the herring fishery.

These craft were to meet for fishing at Yarmouth, Leith, Inverness, Brassey Sound, Kirkwall, Oban, Campbelltown and Whitehaven. But it is rather curious that the Scottish fishing was abandoned to foreigners, who brought in the catches, and then the fish were exported to the British West Indies as food for slaves; but from 1809 the Scottish fishing began to prosper once more. During the nineteenth century the rights of the European States over their territorial waters were defined, for the constant quarrels between the French and British fishermen as to where they could dredge for oysters off the coast were somewhat of a nuisance.

It is since the Sea Fisheries Act of 1868 that all fishing vessels have been compelled to be registered and licensed, and then in 1886 was instituted a Fishery Department in the Board of Trade. The twentieth century has been notable for the way steam and motors have gradually begun to take the place of sailing craft. The steam drifters are able to follow the herring down the coast, but the big steam trawlers are the principal fishing craft in the British Isles today. During the war most of the British steam fishing craft were taken up by the Admiralty for mine-sweeping or anti-submarine work, but by the year 1921 the national fishing had recovered so much that the total landings amounted to over £16,000,000. It is from the North Sea trawlers that most of the fish still comes, and of this a considerable quantity is caught by the trawlers from Hull and Grimsby.

One unfortunate result of the war has been the loss of the Russian and much of the German trade; for in 1913 the United Kingdom exported £5,500,000 worth of cured and salted herring, of which Russia and Germany together took 80 *per cent*. Today from Hull alone there are about 250 steam trawlers fishing and employing about 3000 hands aboard. If you add to this the number of steam, motor and sailing fishing craft from the other ports, it is at once obvious that these fleets form a very considerable portion of the Mercantile Marine.

We may take Hull as representative of modern fishing, but it is only as the result of centuries of experience. Certainly as far back as 1535 the quantity of fish there landed was considered so important as to require an Act of Parliament to regulate the trade. Perhaps the least known was the very important Hull whaling trade, which was carried on for two and a half centuries until about 1868, when, owing to the scarcity of whales, the industry died out, the last whaling voyage being made by the *Truelove*, which had been built in Philadelphia 104 years previously. This vessel made seventy-two whaling voyages, during which she took about 500 whales, and besides these activities filled in the time by general trading, in the Oporto wine trade, and even as a "Letter of Marque."

Other whalers also went to the Arctic from Whitby, Scarborough and London. You may guess how important was the industry when we state that in the year 1821 no fewer than sixty-one whalers left Hull, thirty-two for the area between Greenland and Spitzbergen, and twenty-nine for the Davis Straits.

But there was still another school for seamanship, and it was one of the most important sections of the Mercantile Marine, for two reasons: it not merely trained some of our finest officers and men, but it was until late in the nineteenth century a wonderful fleet of coasters, which passed away only at the coming of the steam collier. We refer to those brigs which used to bring coal from the Tyne to the Thames. These little two-masted vessels were manned by crews who were paid by the voyage. The result was that they were interested in making a quick passage. A contemporary writer, who was himself a privateer for a time, regarded these collier crews as the most perfect in working their ships in narrow channels, as the East Indiamen were the finest in the open seas.

This was in the eighteenth century, but from the time of the Stuarts these Geordie brigs had been plying their trade and building up a fine body of seamen who formed a kind of pool from which ocean-going ships could obtain officers and crews for bolder enterprises. In this branch of the Mercantile Marine the famous discoverer, Captain Cook, learnt his seamanship, which was to lead to such important events. You may remember that whilst still in his teens he became apprenticed for three years in 1746 to the Whitby owners of the 450-ton vessel which carried coal from Newcastle to London, and after two years he served for a time in the 600-ton collier *Three Brothers.* He then served aboard her in the Norwegian and Baltic trades. In the seventeenth century these "coal cats," as they were called, were sometimes three-masted vessels with square mainsail, square foresail, lateen mizzen, and sometimes a main top-sail, but of course no triangular headsails, which did not come in until later.

Captain H.Y. Moffat, who was born in 1844 and served as a boy in the collier-brig *Premium*, has published some interesting facts illustrating this kind of seafaring. His pay was £8—not a week, nor a month, but a year. The second year he was to have £10, and the third year £12. Each of these brigs carried a couple of boys, though the rest of the crew were still paid by the voyage. They lived in a dirty, dark, small fo'c'sle, and during the summer the brig would often run coals across to Hamburg and Rotterdam, but in the winter to London from South Shields. If the surroundings were hardly ideal for a boy, and the pay utterly inadequate, it was a splendid chance for him to learn his seamanship in a rough school. If the brig had a head wind anywhere between Yarmouth and London—that is to say, among all those shoals, these lads were kept busy heaving the lead all the time night and day; for in those times there were no gas-buoys.

As to the men, they knew their job perfectly, but they could neither read nor write. They went aboard the ship with their marlin-spike, pricker, palm, rubber, sail-hook, needles, etc., and even with a well-scrubbed handspike for the windlass. Many of the modern, dry-nursed steamship seamen, better educated and better fed though they are, would have no right to be reckoned in the same category of efficiency as these rough mariners, who still used the old-fashioned hour and half-hour sand-glasses in their brigs. It was one of the most glorious sights to see a fleet of these colliers beating up the Thames.

A waterman was always employed to assist each brig working up the river, and he would come aboard anywhere between Woolwich and Greenwich. If they were beating up with the flood tide, there might be fifty or a hundred brigs all of a bunch, and it would often happen that a brig could not fore reach because of the colliers just ahead. The waterman would therefore put the helm down, let her come up into the wind, and shake, but not so long as to lose way. This was known as a "waterman's nip," and with great care he could make the brig take as long to reach from one side of the river to the other as would allow the crew time to eat their dinner. The collier crews were the smartest men afloat for breaking out the anchor, for the reason that in working their way in and out of so many narrow channels they frequently had to bring up. It was always said that whenever an ex-collier's crew shipped aboard another vessel the windlass required only half the men to work it.

Thus, everywhere the mariner in his own particular sphere was an expert at his job, and though he could never suspect it, he was making history, helping on the development and civilisation of the world. It was a lawless, irreligious, even blasphemous age in which he lived, and it is easy enough to criticise him for his wild excesses. But, having regard to the morals of the time, his poor pay, the disgraceful conditions of service, and the hard life which he was compelled to endure, is it to be wondered at that when he came ashore he was dragged into debauchery? The responsibility rests largely on those who enriched themselves by his bravery, his seamanlike skill and devotion to duty. There is not one of us today who is not a debtor to these old-time mariners for what they have done on our behalf, no matter what their ship.

CHAPTER 12

The Sail-Carriers

If you set aside the forty years from 1837 to 1877 you cover the period which is unsurpassed for the glories of the sea. It is a period when the Mercantile Marine in every ocean rose to such a standard of seamanship as was never seen before nor will ever be witnessed again. It is a time when the triumph of the shipwright and the skill of the sailor combined to bring about the golden age. Every log-book, ship-illustration or reminiscence that bears on this epoch should be regarded with the utmost care and preserved for the wonderment of posterity, for at present we are living so close to this epoch that we hardly appreciate its worth. Those who come after us will rightly envy us for having seen at least some of the ships and spoken with those who handled them. For it was a time when wooden ships were run by men of iron.

The traditions inherited from the old East India Company after the latter had lost its monopoly in India and China were too noble and inspiring to be dissipated at once. The high grade of officers and men remained for a long time a standard, especially when the captain of an East Indiaman even as late as about 1830 was making anything between £6000 and £10,000 a voyage. So, too, the Blackwall yard still retained its name for building the best ships. And though they had ceased to construct the stately but slow vessels which had been good enough as long as the monopoly lasted, a big advance came in the year 1837, when Richard Green launched the 818-ton *Seringapatam*. She was, in fact, the first of a new order of things. In her the double stern and galleries were abandoned, and owing to her finer lines she became famous for her quick and regular passages to the East, and was destined to be the model for many vessels to follow.

It was such men as Green, Wigram, Somes, Dunbar, Baines and

others who built up the Mercantile Marine after the East India Company left the sea; for these men saw their grand opportunity, and seized it. Most of these purchased some of the best of the company's ships. The *Earl of Balcarres*, for instance, was sold for £10,700, and she voyaged for fifty-two years before she became a hulk. The same price was paid for that fine ship the *Thames*; the *Lady Melville* fetched £10,000, the *Buckinghamshire* £10,550 and others realised between £4000 and £10,000. In certain cases the company, seeing their approaching fate, began to sell as far back as 1830.

Some of the captains, officers and men from the honourable company were now taken on by these enterprising new ship-owners about to enjoy the benefits of free trade. But not more than one-fifth of these "old-timers" changed over to the new regime, at any rate straight away. Why? Firstly, these private owners were not too anxious to employ a personnel who had been accustomed to work in ships where expense had not been of the first consideration. Secondly, some officers thought it beneath their dignity to serve in "free trade" vessels, and in any case their remuneration could not be as high as had been possible during the company's extravagant existence. So the captains and officers appealed to their late employers for pensions.

They had entered the East India Company's service expecting provision for life, but now they found themselves awkwardly placed. Not without reluctance the company eventually decided to grant compensations to all commanders and officers who had been in their employ for five years from April 22, 1884. Every commanding officer therefore received £1500 and the other officers received proportionate amounts. But, in addition to this, each commander also received £4000 for three unexpired voyages, £3000 for two voyages and £2000 for one voyage, which they would have made had they continued in the service.

Nor was that all; for those commanders who had served for ten years were given a pension for life of £250 a year, the chief mates getting £160 a year, and so the scale ranged down to the carpenters and gunners. The only condition was that these assured the company of their inability to obtain further employment, and that any income which they possessed was to be in abatement of these pensions. Thus, to the very end, the old East India Company treated its officers and crews very handsomely, especially when we remember the value of a sovereign in those days.

The *Seringapatam* was the first of those famous Blackwall frigates which were the direct descendants of the defunct East India Company. The last of the series, also built by Green's Blackwall yard, was the *Melbourne* (afterwards well known as the *Macquarie*), launched in 1875. Most of this historic fleet were built at the Blackwall yard, at Smith's Tyne yard, at Sunderland or in India, but especially at Blackwall. They were all high-class ships which were run in a high-class manner. The discipline was strict, the personnel was excellent, and they were in every way worthy successors of the old monopolists. If you talk to any of the officers still alive who served in these Blackwallers, or read their reminiscences, you will understand at once that it was thought an honour to be allowed into this new service.

These ships differed from any other merchant vessels in that they carried midshipmen and not apprentices. These midshipmen were drawn from the same families who supplied officers to the Royal Navy, and were known as "young gentlemen." Very often in the case of a country rector who had two sons, you find the eldest going into the navy and the younger into a Blackwall frigate. If a guardian could get a boy into one of these ships, there was no further cause for worry: a fine career was assured. He went to sea in what were happy ships and he gradually rose in his profession until he was making about £5000 a year in the case of the best captains. The guardian or parent had to pay a premium of £60 a voyage for the young midshipman, but those were the days when the commanding officers were the finest navigators in the world and had time to instruct the aspirant. It was a life totally different from that of a modern apprentice.

For some time the officers in these ships were allowed to wear the lion and crown of the East India Company on their uniform buttons, but eventually the house flags of the companies were substituted. A great deal of the old dignity and semi-naval routine were retained in this new service, with action stations and sail-drill. For they were frigate-built and carried guns, so that they could readily be turned into corvettes and be useful fighting units. In an interesting little book entitled Reminiscences of a Blackwall Midshipman, published some years ago, Mr. W. I. Downie remarked with pride:

It was a fine service and afforded a good opening for younger sons, whose elder brothers were in the Army or Navy, but
whose parents could not very well spare the means to dispose
in the same way of all their sometimes numerous progeny.

He himself joined up in the 'sixties, having considered himself disappointed at not entering the Royal Navy, but lucky to obtain a berth as midshipman in Green's Blackwall frigate *Trafalgar*, and bound to India. This ship was built in the year 1848, and was of 1038 tons, her construction being of teak.

When lying at anchor with a few guns on her maindeck and her boat-booms swung out and boats in the water, she might be taken for a frigate, even by a seafaring man, but for the house flag at her main. She had painted ports, square yards and enormous whole topsails. In such a ship no officer or man dared address a superior on duty without saluting. It was because of this excellent discipline and semi-naval character that these well-found ships created such a fine pride of service among its personnel.

We shall speak presently of the other development in shipping which was to proceed collaterally with the Blackwallers, but it may be mentioned here that the latter frequently used to race in the 'sixties against the clippers met on the high seas. Downie mentions that these frigates often were able to hold the clipper ships, especially in hard winds, for though the Blackwallers had high bulwarks and heavy sterns, which made them in comparison look clumsy, yet underwater they had fine lines.

Every known device was resorted to in the effort to squeeze out an extra half-knot, and the third mate of the Blackwaller would be sent down with a gang of men to roust the lee cable out of the chain locker and range it along the weather side of the deck. The fourth mate would take another gang to pump fresh water out of the lee tanks into those of the weather tanks that were empty. In light winds the hose would be taken aloft to wet the sails—the old dodge of making the canvas hold the wind better. Nor did they hesitate to race even against such flyers as the crack clippers *Taeping* and *Fiery Cross*, and in one instance they competed with another sailing ship and beat her home by twenty-four hours; and this after racing for 16,000 miles! Yes, they were sail-carriers in those days. The Mercantile Marine was full of expert seamen.

This *Trafalgar*, for instance, carried, besides her commander, five mates, several midshipmen, a full crew, a bo'sun and his two mates, carpenter, sail-maker, fiddler and cooper. The last two would seem strange to a modern apprentice, but the former used to sit on the capstan and fiddle while the hands were heaving up the anchor with an endless "messenger," and would provide the music for hornpipes danced in the second dog-watch. The cooper was a necessary rating, for casks and barrels were used a good deal, and when not wanted were taken to pieces and reconstructed as required. The midshipmen received their occasional invitations to dine with the captain, as today in the naval service. Sundays and Thursdays were the occasions when there was champagne at the captain's table, and a midshipman thought himself lucky if his turn to be invited occurred on one of these days.

The voyage was begun by the ship being towed out of dock down to Gravesend, where she brought up for twenty-four hours to enable the crew to get over their final shore carouse. The captain—in this case a tall, thin man wearing an eyeglass, himself a scientist and a great authority on the law of storms—would come on board, and the tug would take the ship down to the North Foreland and then cast off. If it was a fair wind the Blackwaller would then carry on down Channel. If it was foul she would anchor and wait for a slant in the Downs. In spite of their sailorlike, alcoholic weakness, these hands were very fine fellows, specially selected, who had sailed in the old East Indiamen or Blackwallers since boyhood, and very rarely did they ever serve in other ships. There was, then, practically continuity of employment, and it is the lack of this which in the twentieth century is the weakest element of the Mercantile Marine.

In these ships there was nothing slovenly, and everyone had to be correctly and smartly uniformed. The officers' cap in those days had the old-fashioned peak at right angles, like that still worn by the officers of the Dutch navy today. Every morning the captain's steward would convey to the midshipmen the instructions as to what rig was to be worn, as, for instance, in fine weather blue jackets, white waistcoats and trousers. In many other merchant ships there was trouble with the crew, which consisted of a mixture of pier-jumpers, gaol-birds and the riff-raff of all the European ports; but it was seldom that the Blackwall men gave any trouble. Every Sunday there was service on the poop in fine weather, or in the saloon when the weather was bad, and all hands were supposed to attend. In harbour the Blackwall ships always looked smart and clean, with yards squared to mathematical precision like a naval frigate.

As a sign of mourning the custom was to paint all the white parts of the ship a pale blue, such as the white ribbon round the hull, the lower masts, the boats, and so on. There were some ships in which the discipline was stricter than in others, according to whether the captain was more disposed towards man-of-war fashion. Those ships which ran to India were more strict in their discipline and more formal in their routine than the vessels which sailed to Australia. In the former the passengers consisted chiefly of army officers and their families, or civil servants going out to take up their appointments, or of consumptives voyaging for their health. But in the Australian ships life was more easy-going, with concerts, theatricals, dances, and even bazaars. In both ships there was a good deal of fraternising and philandering between the younger officers and the eternal feminine, which was natural enough during those long voyages.

The late Captain W. B. Whall, who died not long since, served as a midshipman in the Blackwaller *Hotspur* during the 'sixties, and fortunately has left behind in his *School and Sea Days* some interesting recollections. The commander of this famous 1000-ton East Indiaman was Captain Henry Toynbee, F.R.G.S., F.R.A.S., uncle of Arnold Toynbee, the social economist and philanthropist. Whall describes how, after the *Hotspur* had anchored off Gravesend, the captain would be received on board in true naval style. This commanding officer, who, by the way was uncle to Sir Robert Baden-Powell, the famous scout, will always be remembered for his amazing skill as a navigator.

Captain Whall said he recollected on one occasion when the *Hotspur* had been ninety days out of sight of land, and had sailed over three oceans bound for Calcutta direct, Toynbee came up on deck about 8 p.m. and told the chief officer to send a man up to the foretopsail yard and to order him to look two points on the starboard bow, and he would then see the Lower Floating Light. The hand had barely got his head over the sail when he cried from aloft: "Light two points away on starboard bow." And this was without having sighted anything since the Lizard!

In contrast to this fine ability of an East Indiaman navigator must be placed the rough-and-ready methods of those fine but ignorant skippers of the fruit-trade schooners which were built and sailed like yachts and went down as far south as the Azores. Often when full-rigged ships were blown by easterly gales from the western end of the English Channel as far west as the Fastnet, these splendid little fore-and-afters would be able to make excellent passages to windward. In old waterside inns of the West country you may still see pictures of these ships with the canvas cut in realistic fashion to obtain verisimilitude. They made wonderfully fast passages, and they were most perfectly handled, but the captains, not being capable always of working out their longitude, used to hail any passing ship and hang out a blackboard with the question: "What is your longitude?"

Such a ship as the *Hotspur*, well manned, well navigated, would go round the Cape and land her forty passengers in Calcutta within three months. They would come aboard at Gravesend with their own cabin furniture, but included in the fare was an ample supply of liquor. Often the charge for a stern cabin for a man and wife would be £300 from Calcutta to England, and the ship would have also probably 500 troops aboard, or a total of 600 souls. The decks would be encumbered with sheep, hay, potatoes, bananas, hen-coops, and yet if any disaster had occurred there was accommodation in the boats for not more than about 100.

Whall, who served in these ships for ten years, never once saw a Blackwaller heave-to in a heavy gale. But that was because they were well found and so well manned under the best commanders. In those days the sailor ashore loved his grog too much, and when he left the ship at the end of a voyage with probably £40 on him, he would proceed to get drunk, then perhaps someone in the East End would drug him, and finally, when he awoke up next day he would find himself without so much as a penny. But at sea he was the best fellow in the world, well-disciplined, able to go aloft in the heaviest weather to hand or reef a sail and lay out on a yard. He was an expert at the wheel or with the lead or marlin-spike, and a captain knew that his men could be relied upon from the moment the ship left Gravesend. It was thus that such ships as *Flying Cloud, Sovereign of the Seas, James Baines* and *Marco Polo* could on occasions reel off their eighteen knots, or 420 knots in the twenty-four hours. In fact during the 'fifties the sailing ships could make passages as fast as any mail steamer afloat.

Everyone who has had command of vessels and men realises how important is the spirit of emulation and the pride of ship and service. Whall, the son of a rector, remarked that all who served in these ships looked down on the officers of the Liverpool contemporary sailing ships as being less polished and wearing no uniform, though he ad-mitted they were perhaps smarter sailormen than the Blackwallers. In his memoirs *My Life at Sea,* that experienced mercantile officer, Commander W. C. Crutchley, R.N.R., says of a certain renowned clipper ship:

> The officers and men of that craft considered themselves very
> superior beings to those who had not the good fortune to sail
> under the blue St. Andrew's Cross; but they, in their turn, were
> looked down upon by the men sailing in the ships of Green,
> Dunbar, Wigram and Smith. In those days it would have re-

quired a very careful M.C. to give the varying grades of the Merchant Services their due order of preference.

It was the same at Southampton at one time between the officers of the Royal Mail and the P. & O. Lines, who would not foregather on any account, owing to their mutual jealousies. But those were the days when ship-love and pride of service were more accentuated than to-day. And yet in even some of the contemporary crack steamships there was plenty to find fault with, and Crutchley, who served in the Union liner *Roman*, which ran to South Africa, complains that even in that ocean steamship there was neither engine-room telegraph nor standard compass; for orders were shouted down the engine-room skylight, and the ship was steered from right on the poop, with a binnacle on either side, that on the starboard being the one used for navigating.

We have digressed from our main theme in order to show the spirit which actuated the Mercantile Marine at that important period which followed the abolition of the monopoly and saw the numbers of shipyards, ships and mariners rapidly increasing, thanks to freedom and competition. It is now time for us to watch this progress in detail. If we compare the *Seringapatam* with one of the East India Company's ships of say 1826, we can see indeed more points of resemblance than of difference. Both are frigates, each has a bluff bow and heavy stern that remind us of the Stuart ships, yet in the new type inaugurated by *Seringapatam* it meant a daring advance to omit the heavy double stern and quarter galleries. She still retained her ship rig, her white ribbon, her square ports and her high-steeved bowsprit, but in her was the first break, architecturally, with the olden times. The sailing ship was now in a new era.

Even in the very year of Queen Victoria's accession. Money Wigram launched for the Australian trade the 293-ton *Emit*, for this was beginning to open as an important lane of commerce. And in that same year the yard built such different ships as the 461-ton whaler *Active* and the 621-ton steamer *Neptune*, the latter for the General Steam Navigation Company. It was a couple of years later that they launched the 852-ton *Earl of Hardwicke* for Richard Green. This ship was originally fitted with paddles and 100-horse-power engines to be used in calms, but they were found unsuitable and removed in the following year. And then in 1839 they launched the *Owen Glendower*, which was such a splendid sailing ship that foreign merchant-men used to salute her with the respect as for a man-of-war. She was a sister ship of the *Earl of Hardwicke*. In that year, too, they built the Opium clipper *Moa*

PICTURE OF S.S. NORTHUMBERLAND

for Jardine, Mattheson & Co., though we shall come to the clipper ships presently. Three years later the Blackwall yard launched the two magnificent 1223-ton flush-decked, frigate-built sister ships *Queen* and *Prince of Wales*, as well as the 449-ton *Sylph*.

And here we come to another severing of olden ties, for this was the last ship which was ever built by the firm of Green, Wigrams & Green. In the following year the partnership expired, a wall was built through the yard, and the western portion was made over to Money, Wigram & Sons, whilst the eastern half became the property of Richard and Henry Green. Sentimentally it seemed a pity that after all those years the separation should have taken place; but, as already foreshadowed, it was bound to come, owing to the difference in interests. The firm had become individually interested in ship-owning, and not collectively. Thus Wigram never owned so large a fleet as Green, and where a firm is divided against itself obviously it must come to an end before long.

Richard Green and Henry Green went on building and increasing their ownership until the discovery of gold in Australia, when they launched many ships to cope with the rush. Richard Green did not die until 1863, and just before his death one of his ships had made a voyage to China. In his life he did much to improve the Mercantile Marine, and it was he who was the chief mover and first chairman of what was originally known as the Thames Marine Officers' Training Ship, better known today as H.M.S. *Worcester*. In the year 1922 this ship celebrated its sixtieth anniversary, and during its existence has been able to turn out 3000 officers for the Mercantile Marine, of whom so many distinguished themselves during the Great War. Thus, directly through the Blackwall yard there is an intimate connection between the merchant ships of the time of Queen Elizabeth and those liners of today.

The two finest ships in the Mercantile Marine of 1851 were the East Indiamen *Marlborough* and *Blenheim*, owned by Messrs. T. & W. Smith, who had begun running ships to the East soon after the monopoly had gone, in competition with Green and Wigram. It was the gold-diggings of South Australia and Victoria from 1851 onwards which made a sudden demand for shipping passengers out from England: in fact by 1853 the demand was greater than the supply. But the only suitable vessels available for first- and second-class passengers were these famous Blackwall frigates, and the Greens were thus in a position to transfer some of their large fleet from the Calcutta to the

PICTURE OF AUXILIARY S.S. KENT

Australian trade. Money Wigram, not having yet become a large ship-owner, began to build for this Melbourne trade.

The Blackwall frigates were devoid of sheer, had long poops, short maindecks, and were beautifully built of picked teak and oak. Green's ships were not as sharp-ended as Smith's or Wigram's, but Somes' and Dunbar's were real old-fashioned, clumsy-bowed craft. The fastest of Green's ships were the *Alnwick Castle, Clarence, Windsor Castle* and *Anglesey*. The fastest of Wigram's fleet was the *Kent*, The old East India Company's influence for a time so dominated these Blackwall frigates that dignity, comfort and safety first were rather the mottoes of the fleet, unlike the clipper ships, always snugging down for the night. Some of the best-known Green ships were the 835-ton *Madagascar*, built in 1837, the 852-ton *Earl of Hardwicke*, already mentioned, built in 1838, but afterwards wrecked on the South African coast in 1863; the *Owen Glendower*, built in 1839, the *Agincourt* (958 tons), in 1841, the *Prince of Wales* (1223 tons), in 1842, the *Monarch* (1444 tons), in 1844, the *Alfred* (1291 tons), in 1845, the *Barham* (934 tons), in 1846. *The Prince of Wales* and *Queen* of 1842 were both 1223-ton ships, the former built for Green and the latter for Wigram at the Blackwall yard. Pierced for fifty guns and flush-decked, they were ready with their crew of seventy-eight each to be turned into naval corvettes at once.

The *Anglesey*, built in 1852, of 1018 tons, holds the record for having made the biggest day's run by a Blackwaller. This was 380 miles, and her passage from Melbourne to the Start in seventy-nine days with a crew of forty-six was a remarkable achievement. Wigram's 927-ton *Kent*, built in 1852, was invaluable during the gold rush to Australia. She was one of the crack sailing ships in history, and actually beat the tea-clippers. It was a great innovation when, in 1866 and 1868 respectively, the Blackwall yard built the 1451-ton *Superb* and the 1458-ton *Carlisle Castle*, for both were of iron, and owing to Richard Green's prejudice against iron the firm had to wait until after his death to discard teak. The former became a popular passenger ship to Melbourne; and the last of these famous Blackwall frigates was the *Melbourne*, built for the Greens at the Blackwall yard in 1875 as the finest iron passenger sailing ship in the world. Of 1857 tons and 269·8 feet long, her passenger accommodation was excellent—a great difference from the old East Indiamen.

Until 1887 *Melbourne* sailed regularly to the Australian port of the same name, and was then bought by Messrs. Devitt & Moore, who

PICTURE OF S.S.NORFOLK

changed her name to *Macquarie*. In 1897 she was used as one of this firm's cadet ships, six years later she was sold to the Norwegians and changed her name to *Fortuna*, and these owners eventually sold her, so that now she is used as a hulk in Australia. So ended one interesting period in one of the most important developments of the Mercantile Marine. The combination of personal interest on the part of builder and owner; the great pride in the ship not merely as a money-maker, but as a thing of beauty and queen of the sea; the ability of officers and men serving under a captain who was anxious to maintain the dignity of his line—all these brought about a high standard of seafaring which was thoroughly let down when owners without consciences sent crews to sea in ill-found steam coffin-ships. The fine, historic reputation of the Merchant Service received a shock, the best men were attracted by other walks in life, and so for a while the standard deteriorated.

There are many who believe, rightly, that the Mercantile Marine of any country could and should be run with fixity of employment and the same lofty standard as the fighting navies. If that were done, the grade of officers and men would be as high as it was in the days of the East Indiamen. Let it be realised what a nation's merchant ships mean to the country, and then the public will concede it proper respect and give to that service its best sons.

CHAPTER 13

Cracking-on

We have seen in the development of our subject that it was only after many centuries that the accommodation of the passenger aboard ship was ever considered. We have noticed how the ship was built primarily not for speed, but for carrying the maximum of cargo with the greatest safety. But now there comes into our story the desire for speed as the dominating factor, far more important than any other consideration, and it is in the clipper ships that we get the first merchant vessels that were constructed to cross the seas with the utmost despatch.

It is to North America that this is due. Whilst our bluff, dignified, heavy East Indiamen were slowly making their last voyages before the China monopoly was to come to an end, a remarkable ship, built by her owner regardless of cost, was to appear in Baltimore. This was the *Ann McKim*, of 493 registered tons. This flush-decked vessel came out in 1832. She was very fast, but had small carrying capacity, and was the first clipper ship ever built, and having regard to the daring improvement which America had made in frigates and privateers, it is not surprising that this fast type of merchant ship should come from the same country. The contrast, indeed, between the old East Indiamen and the young clippers is exactly what exists between the Old World and the New Convention was put aside, shipbuilders thought out problems for themselves and had the courage to put their convictions into hulls.

But the first real out-and-out clipper ship was the *Rainbow*, which was launched at the beginning of 1845 in New York. She was a 750-ton vessel with hollow lines at the bows, and her greatest breadth much further aft than had been thought practicable. When constructed, she turned out to be a handsome vessel, exceptionally quick, and she was the fastest vessel in the world. But after trading some time out to China, she was lost in 1848, probably off Cape Horn. Now the cause of attraction towards China at first was the trade in opium. It is not to the credit of British, American or Parsee firms that this pernicious drug was imported into China, where it had been declared illegal by the Government as far back as 1796; but this illicit trade certainly did much to develop fast-sailing ships.

But besides the opium, there was the China tea trade after the East India Company's monopoly had run out, and happily this did even more than the opium to improve the evolution of the quickest fleet of ships under sail that the world has ever seen. In 1846 the 890-ton *Sea Witch* was launched in New York, and she made a wonderful series of voyages to China and back, her best day's run being 358 miles, which was far superior to that of any contemporary steamer. Then came such celebrated American clippers as the *Samuel Russell*, 940 tons, the *Memnon*, 1068 tons, and others. The American trade with China was so important that in one year forty-one ships with tea, silk and spices reached New York from China. The American clippers were certainly the fastest ships of the period, and the *Sea Witch* was still to hold the record for a long time.

But now come two important events which were to have noteworthy results on the Mercantile Marines of the world. The first of these was the repeal of the British Navigation Laws in 1849, and the second was the rush in that same year to California, caused by the discovery there of gold in 1848. We will deal briefly with these factors and pass on. Considerable opposition was made to this repeal, and indeed the first result was that the tonnage of British shipping entering British ports largely decreased and that of American shipping increased. After a few years this competition proved a stimulus to both countries, but especially it caused British owners to wake up in the Atlantic, as the introduction of competition into the Eastern route had already done so much good.

During the 'forties and 'fifties the American Mercantile Marine was in many respects superior to the British, for the reason that the baneful monopoly had caused a kind of self-satisfaction, and therefore no progress to speak of. The long series of Navigation Laws beginning in 1651, and the steady, comfortable, close trade to the East, had lulled British shipping into a kind of stupor. It was only when competition was thrown open to the world that British shipping really got going. The first American ship to carry tea from China to England was the

Oriental, which left China in August 1850 and reached the London River ninety-seven days out from Hong-Kong with 1600 tons.

This was the fastest passage which had yet been made to England. As a beautiful, powerful, speedy, well-found ship the like of her had never been met with in the Thames. Those who had never seen anything but the East Indiamen were amazed at the innovation by the United States Mercantile Marine. But the shock did a world of good. The arrival of tea, in an American ship, in record time, from a country where there had been a British monopoly for so long, caused ship-owners and builders furiously to think.

The result was that two ships were ordered to be built at Aberdeen, for during the last few years Messrs. Hall of that port had been building some fast schooners. The *Stornoway* and *Chrysolite* were thus launched, and have been called the first British tea-clippers, though they were less beamy and powerful than the American clippers. The first ship sailed out to Hong-Kong in 102 days, the *Chrysolite* also went out during 1851 in the same time, and on her way home her best day's run was 320 miles, and she even reached fourteen knots. She got to Liverpool in 103 days, after a very fine maiden voyage. Then came increased competition as the result of *Chrysolite's* achievement, for the American Navigation Club challenged the British shipbuilders to a race with cargo on board from England to China and back for £10,000 a side.

This stake was even doubled, but the challenge was unfortunately never accepted by British ship-owners until Richard Green in 1852 built the tea-clipper *Challenger*, which in that year went out to China, and after loading tea at Shanghai, fell in with the American clipper *Challenge*, three times the size of the British ship. From Anjer they raced home with their tea, and *Challenger* beat the *Challenge* into the dock in London by a couple of days. It is only fair to add that British naval architects had an opportunity of learning from American progress in a very direct manner. For *Oriental* had been previously placed into the Blackwall dock and her lines taken off; and now Challenge went in for the same purpose. Thus, the American clipper ships, with their original design, did have a very powerful effect on the future of British shipping.

The competition in the China tea trade continued, the British clippers of this time made the rivalry very keen, and it is always a matter of regret that there never was another real race between the two countries. But now we must see how the California gold affected the clipper. Briefly these are the facts. In 1848 San Francisco was a mere hamlet, but this sudden discovery of a means to wealth caused a tremendous flow of emigration to the West. Everyone wanted to go, and everyone wanted to get there in the quickest possible time. Leaving out the difficulties in those days of transcontinental travel, the only way possible was by means of ships. The American clipper was thus the solution, and they were there- fore built in great numbers and in a small space of time. In fact within four years 160 were launched, and they sailed from New York to San Francisco in the remarkable time of 100 to 120 days.

Here, then, was yet another incentive to the increase of the Mercantile Marine, to the shipbuilders and to those attracted by the sea. It is comparable only to the impetus which we have seen was received by the Elizabethan seamen. There has seldom been in history such an extensive and speedy migration of people, all anxious to get rich quickly. Once again the ship was invaluable in the service of man.

In the year 1849 over 90,000 passengers landed in that San Franciscan hamlet from ships. On the other hand, it became most difficult to get crews to bring the ships back; for the seamen, too, had gone gold-seeking as soon as the ship had anchored. The California clipper period, as Captain Clark says in his *The Clipper Ship Era*, covers the period 1850 to 1 860, and it is during the first four of these years that nearly all the 160 ships were built, most of them being constructed in the neighbourhood of New York and Boston. It is claimed for them that they were the fastest sailing ships which the world ever saw, and the skippers cracked-on because these vessels were able to earn enormous rates if only the passengers could be landed at their port in the quickest time. Everyone was making money—the ship-owner, captain, crew and then the gold-seekers. Ashore the riggers, shipwrights, painters, sail-makers, metal-workers, spar-makers, pump-makers, blacksmiths, carpenters, caulkers were in such demand that there was prosperity for all, and plenty of it. And it is to this period that a good many of the fast-dying sea-chanties can be traced.

What of the crews that manned the American clippers?

"The history of men before the mast on board American ships," says Captain Clark, "is not a history of American sailors, for strictly speaking there have never been any American merchant sailors as a class; that is, no American merchant ship of considerable tonnage was ever manned by native-born Americans in the sense that French, British, Dutch, Norwegian, Swedish, Spanish

124

or Danish ships are manned by men born in the country under whose flags they sail."

This statement was written in 1910, and of course requires some modification today. But the advent of the Californian clippers necessitated getting men from anywhere—some sailors, many others not, and a whole lot of "bad hats" among them. Of the Californian clippers built in 1851 one was the celebrated *Challenge*, already referred to, a vessel of 2006 tons, one of the largest clippers ever built, though absolutely the biggest was the *Great Republic*, built in 1853. This was constructed by Donald McKay, the famous Nova Scotian builder. She was of 4555 tons register, and was the first ship to have an engine merely for hoisting the yards and working the pumps. Rigged with four masts, she had the misfortune to get on fire when nearly ready for sea, but was rebuilt, being the largest merchant ship of her time, though registering now only 3357 tons.

The famous American clipper *Dreadnought* came out in 1853, and voyaged between New York and Liverpool, and on one occasion made this passage in fifteen days twelve hours, and on another occasion in thirteen days eight hours, though she was wrecked eventually off Cape Horn. But the Australian gold discovery in 1851 had the same effect on shipping that the China tea trade and the California gold rush had created. The fastest vessels were required, competition became keen, and there was no time to waste. Those owners, therefore, who had ships that could carry passengers were in a splendid position from the first, for about 300,000 or 400,000 people each year for the next three or four years had to be transported. From America no less than from England these ships sailed away, and there was the same difficulty in Melbourne with the crews as there had been in San Francisco.

For British ship-owners the difficulty was that there was but little accommodation in most ships, so they thought of the American clippers, which had been doing such fine work. James Baines & Co. of Liverpool therefore had the clipper *Marco Polo* built at St. John's, New Brunswick. She was a very handsome ship of 1622 tons, with considerable rise of floor, very fine aft, and she carried a very large spread of canvas. This was the pioneer of the clipper ships for the Australian trade and the first of the Australian Black Ball Line, her passenger accommodation being a great improvement on the ships usually trading to Australia. She left Liverpool in July 1851, and made a record passage in sixty-eight days to Melbourne, and during the ensuing years of the

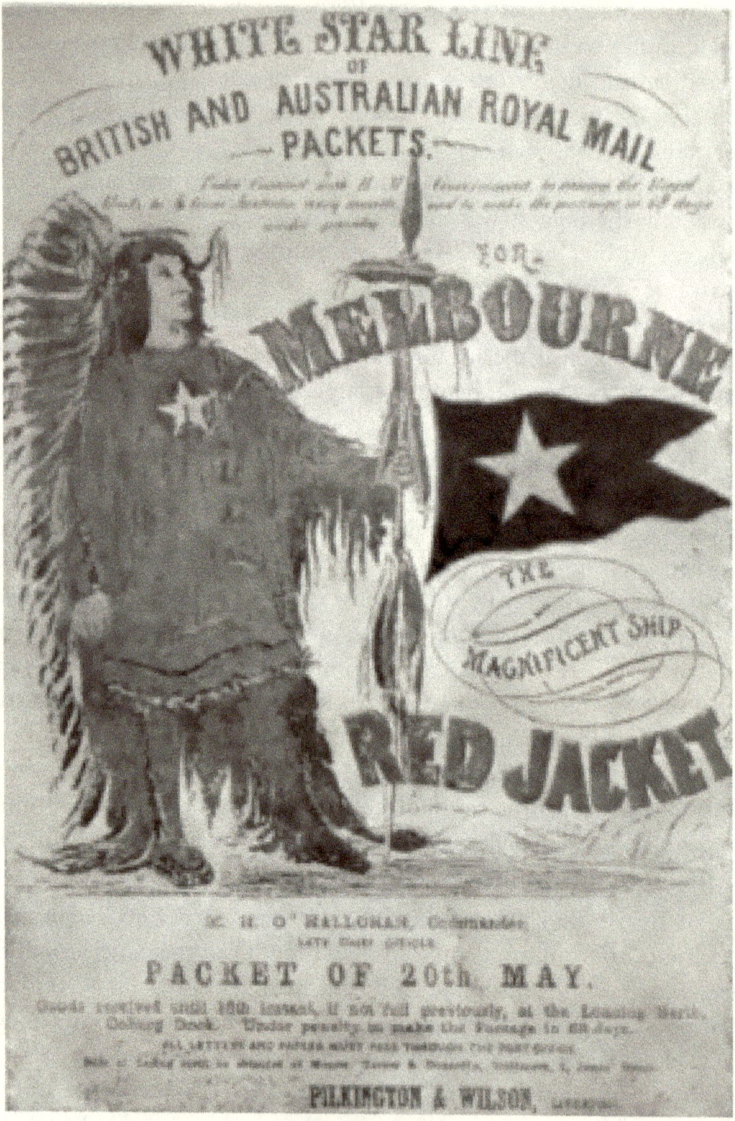

SAILING NOTICE OF THE WHITE STAR CLIPPER *RED JACKET*

gold rush was a very popular and successful ship. The British lines running out to Australia at this time were the White Star (twenty years before they entered the Atlantic steam competition) and James Baines & Co.'s Australia Black Ball Line, just mentioned.

These two firms both had clippers which were built in New England, and one of these, the *Red Jacket*, was for the White Star Line. Named after a noted Indian chief, with a full-length figurehead of him at her bow, this fine ship was one of the most famous of the clippers, and made a fine passage from New York to Liverpool in thirteen days, one hour, when she first came out in February 1854, and on one of the days made 413 miles. During that same year she sailed from Liverpool to Melbourne in sixty-nine days. In his recently published *Reminiscences of a Liverpool Ship-owner*, Sir William B. Forwood has left an interesting account of a voyage he made in this magnificent sailing ship of 2006 tons, three years after she came out.

"On the morning of the 20th November, 1857," he says, "I embarked by a tender from the Liverpool pierhead. It was nearly the top of high water. The crew were mustered on the forecastle, under the 1st Mate, Mr. Taylor. An order comes from the quarter-deck. 'Heave up the anchor and get away.'

'Aye, aye, sir.'

'Now then, my boys, man the windlass,' shouts the Mate, and to a merry chantie:

'In 1847 Paddy Murphy went to Heaven
To work on the railway, the railway, the railway,
Oh, poor Paddy works upon the railway.'

"'The anchor is away, sir,' shouts the chief officer.

"'Heave it a-peak and cathead it,' comes from the quarter-deck, and the tug *Retriever* forges ahead and tightens the tow-rope as we gather way. Bang, bang went the guns, and twice more, for we were carrying the mails, and good bye to old Liverpool, and the crowds which lined the pierhead cheered, for the *Red Jacket* was already a famous ship, and it was hoped she would make a record passage.

"Next morning we were off Holyhead, with a fresh westerly breeze and southerly swell. We were making but poor headway, and shortly the hawser parted. 'All hands on deck,' was shouted by Captain O'Halloran, and a crew of eighty men promptly appeared on deck, for we carried a double crew.

"'Loose sails fore and aft; hands in the tops and cross-trees to see that all is clear and to overhaul gear; let royals and skysails alone:'

"The boatswain's whistle sounded fore and aft as the men quickly took their positions and laid hold of the halyards and braces.

"'Mr. Taylor, loose the headsails.'

"'Aye, aye, sir.' The topsail, courses and topgallant sails were all loose and gaskets made up.

"'Now then, my men, lead your topsail halyards fore and aft, and up with them.' Away the crew walk along with the halyards, and then with a long pull and a pull all together the topsail yards are mast-headed to the chantie:

'Then up the yard must go.
Whiskey for my Johnny,
Oh, whiskey for the life of man,
Whiskey, Johnny.'

With the man at the wheel, keeping his eyes on the weather-luff of the foreroyal, and allowing the sail to be just on the tremble, so as not to lose an inch to windward, the Red Jacket went tearing through the seas, throwing them on either side in a sparkling cascade. By evening the wind had increased, and the captain ordered life-lines to be run fore and aft, and the decks to be sanded and the scuppers to be free. The clipper plunges along, the man at the wheel eases her a few spokes when a squall strikes her, and then bang goes the second jib, blown out of the bolt ropes with the report of a gun. With seas coming in over the forecastle, the hands set another jib, and by this time the clipper is indeed travelling, for by the log she is doing eighteen knots.

During bad weather the fifty saloon passengers and 600 steerage were kept below and the atmosphere was stifling. There was none of the comfort or luxury of a modern steamship, and the clipper was heeling over in a way that would alarm many travellers today. But at last, after sixty-four days, the Red Jacket had made Port Philip Heads, and so a record voyage to Australia.

Those were the days when travelling by sea was romantic and not as monotonous as a railway journey. With the captain cracking-on to make a fast trip, with sails carrying away, spars and gear as well, there was always some sport, some adventure. Between 1850 and the following ten years Prince's Dock, Liverpool, was crowded with fine clippers raising their lofty masts and crossing their great spars. And those were the days of wonderful feats of seamanship. Sir William Forwood says that he remembers seeing the 600-ton Brocklebank sailing

CRACKING-ON

ship *Martaban* come sailing into George's Dock Basin under all canvas. Her halyards were then let go and sails clewed up so smartly that the ship, as she passed the pierhead, was able to throw a line on shore and make fast. Could you beat this for seamanlike skill and discipline?

But it is with the celebrated China tea-clippers from about 1860 onwards that this skill reached such heights of proficiency. British ship-owners no longer found it necessary to have their clippers built in America, and the Merchant Shipping Act of 1854, together with the enterprise learnt in a hard school, as the result of competition, enabled British shipping to go ahead. The California boom, which had produced America's finest clippers, was dead. The great quantities of American timber would soon be not wanted for shipbuilding, now that iron was coming in and steam was replacing sails. But that which gave the final character to the American Mercantile Marine was the outbreak of civil war in 1861 between the North and South. From that it never recovered until the new efforts, begun in 1917, to rebuild a service that had been such a keen competitor during the clipper-ship period.

In the meantime, during the 'sixties and onwards, the British Mercantile Marine, by the enterprise of the ship-owners, the assistance of legislation, the protection of the British Navy, the scientific progress of shipbuilders and engineers, and by the skill and endurance of its officers and crews, regained its supremacy after a stiff fight, and opened up new trade routes in all parts of the world. And this not merely in regard to the big lines, but especially in respect of the tramp steamers going out with coal and bringing back all sorts of essential produce.

The Clyde was gradually beginning to take the place of the Blackwall yard, and this became still more so as the need for coal and iron increased, owing to the fact that the Thames is not convenient to coalfields. It was in 1855 that Steele of Greenock built his first tea-clipper, the *Kate Carnie*, about 600 tons, and thereafter he built, among other beautiful and eye-pleasing ships, the historic *Taeping, Serica, Ariel* and *Sir Lancelot*, all under 900 tons, yet exceedingly fast. From 1855 to 1881 is the comprehensive period of these China tea-clippers, and their evolution should be compared with that of the Blackwall frigates already dealt with. The Steele clippers had a full midship section and fine ends, but some of the other clippers were fined away like the hulls of schooner yachts. Unlike the obstinate Blackwallers, many tea-clippers had a certain amount of sheer. From 1863 both the Clyde and Aberdeen firms launched composite-built clippers, and these were so

SPARS & STAYS

beautifully tight as to require practically no pumping, and so the cargoes of tea arrived in perfect condition.

The British tea-clippers of the period under consideration were smaller than the American clippers, had less sheer, less freeboard, and were more slim and graceful, with decks unencumbered except with small houses; with less heavy spars, less beam, and were designed to carry small cargoes of tea with the utmost despatch. They were a small fleet in numbers, but their excellence was rather in a sustained average speed throughout their voyages than in hourly or daily runs.

The longest day's run by a tea-clipper was 363 miles, and this record was made by *Cutty Sark*, and the only other clipper that could rival her was the *Thermopylae*. These tea-clippers were economical to run, handled by magnificent British seamen, and commanded by captains of great experience, courage and enterprise. The composite construction of wooden planking and iron frames gave these little ships unusual strength, they were ballasted with shingle, and in light weather could utterly outsail a Black Baller, a Californian clipper or a Blackwall frigate. But because of their comparative smallness it is not to be imagined that in heavy weather they could compete with the American clippers of much greater tonnage and freeboard. *Cutty Sark's* rival, *Thermopylae*, being of her own nationality, on one occasion did 358 miles, and *Ariel* 840 miles, in the twenty-four hours.

But these tea-clippers needed proper handling, like sensitive horses, and required to be humoured. Those were the days when the love of ships by owners, captains and crews was something real, when clippers were treated like human beings and given everything they wanted; and their loss often meant the breaking of the owner's heart. The personal relationship between the owner, his ship and captain was something very different from today. Before the advent of limited liability companies and telegraph cables, instructions were given personally by the owner, who would himself come down to see his ship start.

In many cases the captains were financially interested in the ships, and it must be remembered that the best clipper-ship captains were hard to find. Remembering that an owner required neither a mere dare-devil nor one who merely played for safety, but a captain who would crack-on without losing ship or gear, and whilst getting the last ounce out of the ship would know instantly when to ease up, it is obvious that an ideal commander would be a mixture of courage, iron nerve, initiative, driving power, sound judgment based on experience, consummate sea-manlike ability and great physical endurance.

It was when such skippers got command of these lovely little ships that the tea was raced home in such splendid time. They had to watch their ships from hour to hour during the three months' race from China to England, rarely going below, getting very little sleep, and the result was that many eventually broke down. But we must think of them as the keenest lot of captains who ever sailed the seas, and up to every dodge to get the ship home quicker than the other fellow. They looked for risks and accepted them freely, but they were not foolhardy, and they knew just how much their ships could stand. Backed up not by mutinous crews, as was often the case in the American clippers, but by thorough seamen, all British, a captain knew that he could rely on them to aid him in getting the most out of his ship; for they were not less keen than himself, and were betting against the other ships. It meant hard work, but no sailorman will ever grouse at this if he is in tune with the reason. They took a pride in their vessels and were jealous of a ship's honour. Could the same be said nowadays of the crews of steamships? Sentiment in seafaring has a tremendous practical value if only it is appreciated and properly trained.

In his volume *The China Clippers*, Mr. Basil Lubbock says that

. . . .in the heyday of the racing, Foochow was the loading port *par* excellence, and the Pagoda anchorage, just before the tea came down the river, showed perhaps the most beautiful fleet of ships the world has ever seen. The crack ships, which were always the first to load, began to assemble about the end of April; and until the tea came down were all engaged in painting, varnishing and smartening themselves up, and in other ways, such as sheathing over their channels, preparing for the fray. Then what a sight they made when all was spick and span, with their glistening black hulls, snow-white decks, golden gingerbread work and carving at bow and stern, newly-varnished teak deck-fittings, glittering brass and burnished copper. Every ship, of course, had her distinctive mast and bulwark colours.

The tea-clipper *Fiery Cross*, launched in 1860 at Liverpool and wood-built, was to become famous for her fast passages home. It was customary in those days for the first vessel who landed the new teas in England to receive a premium. This vessel won the premium on four occasions. Then in 1863 Steele built the *Serica* and *Taeping*, two of the most famous clipper ships. The former was wood-built and of 708 tons. The latter was composite-built and of 767 tons, and it was in 1865 that two more Steele composite tea-clippers were launched, also to become famous. These were the 853-ton *Ariel* and the 886-ton *Sir Lancelot.* Very beautiful craft they were, and no ship-lover can regard the existing pictures of these handsome craft without a thrill of emotion.

Symmetry, grace, proportion, curves, easy lines as to hull; a good sail-plan, tall masts and fine spars; carrying in light winds all sorts of kites and fancy sails, the supreme test came in the ever-memorable race of 1866, which is one of the greatest events in the whole history of merchant ships under sail. On May 28, 1866, there was a whole fleet of these clippers loading at Foochow. At 5 p.m. *Ariel* began her voyage, by dropping down and anchoring for the night; and then followed the *Fiery Cross, Taeping, Serica* and *Taitsing*, at intervals. On August 12 *Ariel* passed the Cape Verde Islands, next day came *Taeping, Fiery Cross* and *Serica*, the *Taitsing* not passing until the 19th, but she had made up these three days by September 1. On September 5 *Ariel* picked up the Bishop Light, sighted *Taeping*, and the two raced up Channel, doing their fourteen knots. *Ariel* got her pilot at six the next morning off Dungeness, followed immediately by *Taeping*.

In the Downs *Taeping* got the more powerful tug, and thus reached Gravesend nearly an hour sooner, and finally docked twenty minutes before *Ariel*. It was a near thing after racing for three months from one end of the world to the other. *Serica* docked on the same tide. *Fiery Cross* was only about a day later, and *Taitsing* arrived in the river on September 9. And there were plenty more of these races, for the skippers cracked-on and made these clippers do marvellous things through the water.

But in 1868 there was built at Aberdeen the famous clipper *Thermopylae*, 947 tons, a bigger and more powerful ship than the Steele clippers, and a veritable witch at sailing, whether on the wind or to windward, and a wonderful sea boat, too. In November 1868 she started on her maiden voyage from Gravesend, and reached Melbourne in sixty-three days. Mr. Downie, already quoted, whilst a midshipman in a Blackwaller, happened to be in Melbourne when *Thermopylae* came in, and went aboard to look over this new wonder ship.

> "She had immensely square yards," he says, "and most beautiful lines, fore and aft. Her apprentices told me her skipper had driven her all the way, carrying-on tremendously, but her spars and rigging were all new, and of the best material, and stood the severe strain in splendid fashion."

PORT OF LIVERPOOL IN 1798

SCREW S.S. *LADY JOCELYN*

Thermopylae broke records, and in 1869 got home from Foochow in ninety-one days, though *Sir Lancelot* less than a fortnight later arrived after a voyage of only eighty-nine days. But then came the splendid *Cutty Sark*. She is the only one of this long line of tea-clippers still afloat and at work. In the autumn of 1921 she came into the London river, and I was able to go all over her. But she had changed her name to *Ferreira* and was Portuguese-owned and rigged as a *barquentine*. For all that, and the disappointing way in which she was being kept up, she was in excellent condition, with a yacht-like hull, every line of which suggested grace and speed. Composite-built, this 921-ton vessel was a little bigger than *Thermopylae*, and was launched in 1869. Under Captain Moodie this vessel cracked-on, and she could do her seventeen and a half knots, and anyone who has examined her bow and stern will readily believe this.

And here, in the height of their glory, we must now leave these clippers; for the opening of the Suez Canal told owners pretty plainly that the future for them was to leave sail and go in for steam. In 1881 *Thermopylae* made her last passage as a tea-carrier, and all the other clippers had either gone or were out of the running, and used in other trades. Crews began more frequently to go into steamships, famous captains retired, and the younger men, like the crews, preferred the more comfortable life in a mechanically-propelled vessel. But for years the American and British clipper ships were the glory of the Mercantile Marine, as at one time the old East Indiamen had been before the days of healthy competition. The influence of the scientific French architects on the American builders of frigates and privateers is traceable through the clipper ships which followed. Thus mutually one nation is linked with another in the development of that great service which has meant so much for the good of the world.

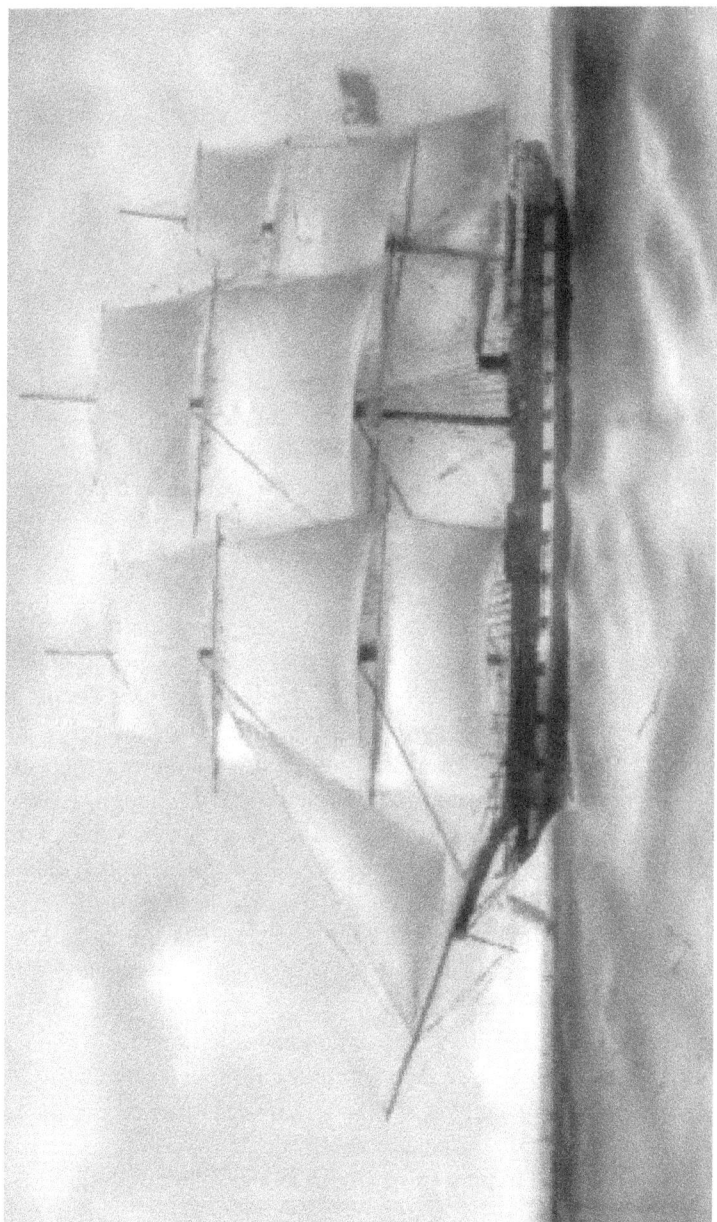

Screw S.S. Indomitable

CHAPTER 14

The Triumph of Steam

The speed of life, the rate of progress, and the development of new ideas have since the beginning of the nineteenth century been so rapid that all the previous history of the Mercantile Marine, as in other spheres of activity, seems ridiculously slow and unduly protracted until we realise that a ship could not become efficient until she had the right type of hull and the correct distribution of sails, nor be able to steam until suitable engines had evolved by invention and long practice.

It is a *cliché* to speak of the "wonderful" nineteenth century, and yet in regard to its effects on the sea services it is but expressing a literal truth. The amazing fact is, that just as the sailing ship was becoming perfect the steamship was beginning to take its place; and just as the clippers had definitely created the golden age of sail, steamers had become reliable, indispensable and destined to make sailing vessels out of date. If steam and iron, and then steel, had not been introduced into marine progress for another hundred years, and the clippers had been allowed to have the seas to themselves, it would have seemed but fair and natural, having regard to the centuries and centuries which had been necessary to bring about, at last, so perfect a creation of man's science, art and bitter experience.

But it was not to be. The story of the steamship, like that of the sailing ship, is one of evolution; but compressed into a few years instead of many centuries. As early as 1736 a steam vessel had been patented by Jonathan Hulls, to be used as a steam tug. It is even said that such a craft was built and experimented with in the following year; but at any rate the experiment was not continued. The essential idea was the use of a single paddle at the stern. Now follows the trend of invention. In 1783 a two-paddle-wheel steam craft, turned by a single horizontal

Lord Yarborough's yacht *Falcon*

steam cylinder, constructed by the Marquis de Jouffroy, actually went ahead for some time against the current of the Saône. For some time Patrick Miller had been experimenting with the old idea of propelling craft by hand-worked paddle-wheels. In 1787 William Symington had obtained a patent for a new steam-engine, and he was now asked to design an engine that would turn these paddle-wheels.

Thus in the autumn of 1788 the engine was put into a double-hulled vessel, no bigger than the smallest yacht, measuring 25 feet long, with 7 feet beam, the engine being geared with chains and the two paddle-wheels being placed between the two hulls, one wheel astern of the other. This curious vessel was actually tried on Dalswinton Loch and was able to do her five miles an hour.

Then in 1801 was built the stern-wheeler *Charlotte Dundas* at Grangemouth, having engines supplied by Symington. She also had a double stern with two rudders controlled by a steering-wheel. She proved her efficiency to the extent of towing a couple of 70-ton, loaded vessels for nearly twenty miles along the Forth and Clyde canal; but as the owners of this waterway feared for the damage done to the banks of the canal, the ship was condemned. We have to look upon these as hardly anything more than interesting experiments, but six years later we see the first real steamship, not in England nor Scotland, but in North America, yet produced by a combination of British and American brains.

This was the *Clermont*, measuring 133 feet long and 18 feet beam, and was produced by Robert Fulton, an American engineer, born in Pennsylvania of Irish parentage. In 1797 he came to Paris, where he devoted his attention to steam navigation, and in 1808 built a small steamboat which went up the Seine. Three years later he went back to America, having seen the trial trip of the *Charlotte Dundas*. He arranged with the British firm Boulton & Watt to make for him the principal portions of a suitable engine, and these were sent across the Atlantic to him and fitted into the wooden ship *Clermont*.

The result was that in 1807 this craft travelled by steam power from New York to Albany up the Hudson, a distance of 150 miles, in thirty-two hours. This was a veritable triumph, and definitely settled the question as to whether steam vessels would ever become of practical utility. It is, indeed, one of the landmarks of history, and when we look on the ocean today and see such mighty steamships as *Olympic, Aquitania, Majestic* and *Berengaria*, to say nothing of the many thousands of smaller steamers all over the world, it is nothing short of remarkable that in little more than a hundred years such a stupendous change should have come about. The advancement of the ship seems suddenly to have been telescoped. But the successive stages were not easy, and there was much to be learnt. In 1811 on the Clyde was launched the *Comet*, a clumsy little thing of forty feet length on the keel, and able to steam five miles an hour by means of one paddle on each side, as in the case of the *Clermont*.

During the next few years paddle-steamers began to be built and introduced on the Clyde, Thames and Mersey. By 1817 a steamer called the *Caledonia* had been taken from the Clyde to the Thames, whence, after receiving new engines, she steamed to Rotterdam. A year later came the 90-ton *Rob Roy*, constructed by William Denny and engined by Napier with thirty nominal horse-power. After running for some time between Greenock and Belfast, she was transferred to the Dover-Calais route, but in the meantime steamer development was proceeding in other parts of Europe. For in 1815 a small craft called the *Elizabeth* was running on the Neva, another steamer was carrying passengers between Cronstadt and St. Petersburg, whilst in Germany the first vessel of this kind to be built was the *Prinzessin Charlotte*, a double-hulled thing with a single paddle-wheel between the hulls. She was running on the Elbe and Spree as early as 1816.

Thus far small steamers had shown their utility for inland waters and for short sea passages; but now comes another important event. In the year 1818 there was built in New York the 350-ton full-rigged ship *Savannah*, but she was also fitted with a low-pressure engine of ninety horse-power, and a couple of paddle-wheels, one on each side. These were so arranged that they could be hoisted on board. In the following year she crossed the Atlantic to Liverpool in thirty days, but this was largely a sailing passage, for she did not use her engines except for eighty hours, and by the time she had reached the Irish coast she had consumed all her fuel. On her return to America her engines were removed and she became a sailing ship simply. Still, for the first time in history a ship had been driven by steam in the Atlantic, and it showed what could be expected presently.

And then came a surprise. In that yard which had been building nothing else but sailing ships since the time of *Elizabeth*, in that yard where the flower of the British merchant fleet had always been constructed, there was now actually being made a steamer! It seemed incredible, but it was true, and it caused a great sensation at the time. In 1820 had been formed the first steamship company, under the title of

CLIPPER SCREW S.S. *HELLENIS*

S. S. *ORINOCO*

the General Steam Navigation Company, and they gave the order for their first steamer to the Blackwall yard of Wigram & Green. This ship was the 401-ton paddler *City of Edinburgh*, for the Edinburgh trade, and she was launched in 1821, the same year as the yard also launched the 1333-ton East Indiaman *Duchess of Atholl*, one of the finest sailing ships of the time. It was significant of the big change that was coming over the Mercantile Marine, though for many a year most of the officers and men heartily despised anyone who deserted sail for steam.

In the following year this same yard launched the 180-ton paddler *King of the Netherlands* for the same owners, and in 1823 they built three more steamers of from 244 to 510 tons. The *City of Edinburgh* had been launched in March, and had caused so much interest that the future *William IV* and *Queen Adelaide* went to look over her and were surprised at the magnificence of her passenger accommodation. The engines were of only 100 horse-power, yet the Press at the time referred to them as "extremely powerful." Then in the following June was launched at Port Glasgow the 420-ton three-masted schooner *James Watt*, which had a long, narrow funnel, about as tall as her mainmast, and a paddle-wheel on either side of the ship driven by engines of the same horse-power as those for the *City of Edinburgh*.

The steamship had thus got a good start, though as regards ocean work the engines were auxiliary rather than the main propelling power. In 1825 the 176-ton auxiliary *Falcon* reached Calcutta *via* the Cape, and the 470-ton *Enterprise* made the same voyage in 113 days, but for 103 days she used steam. This was the biggest test which marine machinery had so far endured. It proved a good deal, and therefore it is not surprising that two years later there were eighty steamers classed in Lloyd's Register, and five years later there were 100. But the Atlantic had not yet been conquered by steam, and when we realise that *Aquitania* was not in commission until 1914, we can well appreciate the rate of progress that was afterwards made. In 1831 a vessel named the *Royal William*, 176 feet long, was built in Quebec, and fitted with engines made by Boulton & Watt that had been sent across the Atlantic. Two years later this ship crossed the ocean to Cowes, having done the 2500 miles in seventeen days, yet there is some doubt as to whether she used her engines throughout the whole voyage.

But the year 1838 was to be remarkable in the story of the Atlantic, for on April 4 there started from Cork the 703-ton paddler *Sirius*, which reached New York on April 22. She had steamed all the way, but it had been a near thing, for her fuel gave out and she had even to burn some of her spars. At one stage of the voyage her captain had to quell a mutiny, for the crew began to assume that the ship would never get across. Twelve hours after her arrival came into New York the four-masted paddler *Great Western*, which had left Bristol on April 7. She was a much larger ship, of 1321 gross tons, and had been specially designed by that engineering genius Brunel to withstand Atlantic weather. On the return voyage she took fifteen days, and *Sirius* seventeen. *Great Western* was a most successful ship, both technically and commercially. At the end of the first year she earned a dividend of 9 *per cent.*, thirty-five guineas being the fare, and she carried 152 passengers. She was not broken up until 1847.

So far no steamer had crossed from Liverpool to New York, though the sailing ships were still doing the voyage in about three weeks, but in 1838 a second *Royal William* accomplished this. She was hardly the kind of paddler to choose for Atlantic work, and had really been built for the Liverpool-Kingstown route. Built and engined at Liverpool, being three feet shorter but two feet wider than *Sirius*, she was thus the first of those steamers to maintain the communication between Liverpool and New York, which has meant so much to the mutual commerce and development of ideas in the two countries.

On April 2, 1839, the three-masted paddler *British Queen* left Portsmouth and reached New York on April 16, or three days quicker than the first *Royal William* had done the journey in the opposite direction under sail and steam. Encouraged by the success of *Sirius*, which had been chartered because the British Queen was not yet ready, the British Queen Steam Navigation Company had also built the sister ship *President*, 1863 tons and 700 horse-power; but after sailing from New York on March 11, 1841, with a few passengers, *President* was never heard of again, and thus the company came to an end.

We have now reached a stage when a change was coming over the Mercantile Marine slowly but without a doubt. A new competition was beginning, yet so far sail was ahead and improving all the time. But from the number of new shipyards which were springing up, and the interest which they and owners were taking in the steamship, it was obvious even soon after Queen Victoria's accession that in the steamship lay the future of the trading and passenger ship.

It is to be noted that during the time of the Honourable East India Company their ships were primarily and essentially freighters. They earned their profits by carrying valuable exports and imports. The few passengers who travelled were officials going out to India in the service of the company, or returning home. Today the finest merchant ships in the world are not freighters, but passenger ships. It is the tramp which has succeeded to the carrying trade of those pioneer ships; and after the Indian monopoly had disappeared, and there came a need for people to go out East, it was quite an innovation to provide more accommodation for passengers. Then the same thing happened in regard to China, but especially with the emigration to Australia. Gradually this element increased, people began to travel all over the world, for business, for administrative reasons, for pleasure; and as the number of passengers increased so the amount of cargo space was encroached upon. Especially was this the case in the transatlantic ships, so that today the principal liners on that route carry practically no cargo beyond mails and the passengers' luggage. Thus, within a hundred years, the needs of the public have entirely altered the characters of the shipping.

It was natural enough that the East should for so long have instigated all the improvements in shipping, for the reason that travellers went to the Orient long before America was discovered, and the East India Company had a continuous need for the best ships. But since the introduction of steam and the rapid progress of the United States, it is the West, and not the East which has always seen the greatest enterprise in shipping. Bigger and better vessels, compound engines, twin screws, triple screws, quadruple screws, turbines, oil fuel, increased speed, luxurious accommodation—all these most important and progressive factors in the Mercantile Marine have come as a result of the Atlantic, and not the Oriental trade.

In reality it is all traceable to the year 1840, though the establishment of Lloyd's Register in 1834,[1] the founding of the Marine Department of the Board of Trade in 1846 and the repeal of the Navigation Laws in 1849 have also to be reckoned as having powerfully contributed to the improvement of British shipping. Some time since I had in my hands the log of the sailing ship *Elizabeth*, which sailed from the Thames in the spring of 1833, arrived in China the following January, left there in March, called at St. Helena in June, then crossed the Atlantic and reached Halifax in August. She was, I believe, the last of the ships owned by the Honourable East India Company to leave China before the monopoly ended.

Now, as showing the interlocking of human affairs, it is interesting

1 By the amalgamation of the Register of Shipping (1760) and the *New Register Book of Shipping* (1799). 176

to observe that at Halifax she went alongside Mr. Cunard's wharf, for he was the East India Company's agent in that port. Curiously, five years previously, in reply to a letter sent to his firm by Messrs. Ross & Primrose, Cunard had written:

> We have received your letter of the 22nd inst. We are entirely unacquainted with the cost of a steamboat, and would not like to embark in a business of which we are quite ignorant. Must, therefore, decline taking any part in the one you propose getting up.

Now in those days the arrangements for postal contracts were in the hands of the British Admiralty, who were so impressed by the wonderful steamship achievements of 1838 that they proceeded to issue circulars inviting tenders for the carrying of American mails by steamers. It so happened that one of these circulars fell into the hands of Samuel Cunard of Halifax, who owned a number of sailing ships trading between Boston, Newfoundland and Bermuda. He had been one of the shareholders of the first *Royal William*, which had crossed in 1833 from Nova Scotia to Cowes. Having read the circular and made up his mind, he came to London in order to raise the required money, but the merchants would have nothing to do with the scheme. From the secretary of the East India Company he obtained a letter of introduction to Mr. Robert Napier, a Clyde shipbuilder and engineer, who in turn introduced him to Mr. George Burns, and the latter introduced him to Mr. David MacIver. Each of these two last mentioned was an expert in the shipping business, and in a few days the necessary capital of £270,000 was subscribed. A tender was then made to the Admiralty for the conveyance of Her Majesty's mails once a fortnight between Liverpool, Halifax and Boston. This was accepted in competition, and a contract was signed for seven years. It was agreed that the service was to be carried on by four ships, that fixed dates of sailings should be adhered to, and that the company should be subsidised to the extent of £81,000 a year.

Thus the famous Cunard Company was founded. Cunard came to London, Burns to Glasgow and MacIver to Liverpool, and to these three men we owe a great deal of the subsequent development of Atlantic shipping and the progress of the Mercantile Marine. The company was at first known as "The British and North American Royal Mail Steam Packet Company," and in the year 1840 these four wooden ships were built on the Clyde and supplied with engines by

Robert Napier. The first was the *Britannia*, followed by the *Acadia*, *Caledonia* and *Columbia*. They were propelled by paddle-wheels, carried 115 cabin passengers and 225 tons of cargo, and they were all approximately 1154 tons, and 207 feet long. Regardless of superstition, *Britannia* began her maiden voyage on a Friday, which happened to be July 4, a day which commemorated another kind of Independence. After a fine trip of eleven days and four hours she reached Halifax, and thence proceeded to Boston, just a fortnight plus eight hours out from Liverpool. The citizens of Boston celebrated the historic event with banqueting and enthusiasm, and thus was forged one of those links which have bound the two nations together for so many years ever since.

Following the precedent of the Cunard Company, the Royal Mail Line in March 1840, obtained a contract to carry the mails in at least fourteen "good substantial and efficient steam vessels" to the West Indies, whither previously the mails had been carried in gun-brigs. The contract was for ten years from December 1841. All the ships were named after British rivers, and they used to depart from Falmouth, the voyage taking from seventeen to eighteen days. It is evidence of the great spread of shipbuilding already that these fourteen ships were built at Northfleet on the Thames, Greenock, Dumbarton, Leith and even Cowes. The fleet cost about £1,000,000 sterling, but the Government gave them a subsidy of £240,000 a year. The undertaking was very successful, and presently Southampton took the place of Falmouth. Then in 1851 the Royal Mail Line extended their service to South America. Gradually the heavy subsidy dropped to £85,000 a year, and was finally abolished in June 1905.

As further evidence of the solid belief which the steamship had now won, it is only necessary to refer to the Pacific Steam Navigation Company, which received its charter in 1840. It is now amalgamated with the Royal Mail Line, but in those days, whilst the latter served the east side of South America, the Pacific Steam Navigation Company served the Pacific coast of that continent by going round through the Magellan Straits. Their two ships the *Chile* and *Peru* were in fact the first two steamers which ever passed through those straits. What a wonderful change since the time of Drake's ships!

But there is still one more important event which belongs to the year 1840, for this was the date when there was incorporated by royal charter the Peninsular & Oriental Steam Navigation Company. The foundation of the Peninsular Company dates back to 1837, and a regular service of mail packets was instituted from London to Lisbon and Gibraltar, though even a little prior to this date its ships had begun running to the Peninsula. The first steamship owned by the Peninsular Company was the 209-ton paddler *William Fawcett*, built in the year 1829, and she ran from London to Lisbon and Gibraltar. In 1840 the line was extended to Malta and Alexandria, and its title changed from Peninsular to Peninsular and Oriental.

There was as yet no Suez Canal, so from Alexandria passengers and goods were sent by the Mahmoudieh Canal to the Nile, whence they proceeded by steamer to Cairo, and from there travelled through the desert on camels as far as Suez. It was thus a laborious business, 3000 camels being employed for transporting a single steamer's loading, every package requiring three separate transfers; and for nearly thirty years this continued until the Suez Canal was opened in 1869.

But this company first sent a steamer to India *via* the Cape in 1842. This was the 1800-ton *Hindostan*, with 500-horse-power engines. In 1844 the P. & O. undertook the mail service from England to Alexandria, and thus from Suez to Ceylon, Calcutta and China. The service between Suez and Bombay was carried on by the East India Company, in order to keep alive their navy, but in 1854 this service was absorbed by the P. & O., who in 1852 had also started a branch line from Singapore to Australia. Then in 1869 came the opening of the Suez Canal, and thus was broken down the last barrier which separated India from the trader. A tremendous impulse was given now to shipping; for the first time vessels need not go round the Cape of Good Hope, and so once again the Mediterranean ceased to be a backwater and the route to the East was now more like what it was before the Portuguese, Dutch and Elizabethan English had begun to undertake their Oriental voyages.

It is interesting to remark that in the same year which saw the opening of the Suez Canal the two fastest clipper ships which ever sailed were both afloat—*Thermopylae* and *Cutty Sark*. The latter made her maiden voyage in the following February. Thus, at a time when sailing ships were passing the Cape at a record speed, the canal was being opened and putting an end to the sail-driven vessel's usefulness after so many centuries, linking it up with Vasco da Gama and earlier.

TWO EARLY MAIL STEAMSHIPS

CHAPTER 15

The Iron and Steel Age

In a very few years, then, the increasing success of the steamer, together with the opening of the Suez Canal and firm establishment of several steamship companies carrying mails east, west and south, gave the glorious sailing ships a blow from which they have never since recovered. Mechanically-propelled craft were now seen everywhere. In 1841 the Blackwall yard launched the 666-ton paddler *Princess Royal* and the 875-ton paddler *Trident* for the General Steam Navigation Company. The latter craft was one of the fastest vessels afloat, and on Queen Victoria's first visit to Scotland this ship so far surpassed the royal yacht in speed that Trident was chartered for Her Majesty's party on the return voyage.

From 1840 to about 1860 the Cunard ships had practically a monopoly of the Atlantic steamship trade, though as long as they used paddle-wheels they were not very serious competitors with the sailing craft. It was the advent of iron and steel, of the high-pressure and compound engines which was to give the steamships the virtues of economy and efficiency and thus a superiority over the old-fashioned craft. From 1850 for the next eight years there was in the North Atlantic a certain amount of opposition from a steamship company called the Collins Line, which had been subsidised by the United States Government.

After a burst of keen rivalry, the Collins Line withdrew from the contest. In 1850 came the Inman Line, which kept up the running for many years until in 1893 it was reorganised and became merged in the American Line. In 1866 was founded the Guion Line, which certainly had a great influence for a time in accelerating the development of the big steamship. And then in 1870 came the White Star Line, which, excepting the Cunard Line and a temporary influence

S.S. TRIDENT

of the two German lines, has done more for the improvement in design and speed and comfort in regard to steamships than all the other companies put together.

We must now see how this all came about. It depended really on two things: first, the use of iron, and subsequently steel, for the building of bigger hulls; and secondly, the invention of the screw propeller to take the place of the old-fashioned paddle-wheel. Briefly how this came to pass is as follows. As far back as 1821 a Mr. Aaron Manby had built an iron craft 120 feet long and 18 feet wide, and she steamed from London to Paris, being employed for the next twenty years on the Seine. She was thus the first iron ship to put to sea, and was called the *Aaron Manby*, after her builder. Then in 1832 Laird & Co. of Birkenhead built the 148-ton paddler *Lady Lansdowne* for the trade between England and Ireland. But it was not until 1843 that the first really large iron ship, the famous *Great Britain*, was built, intended as an improvement on the *Great Western*.

But before we speak of the *Great Britain* we must see something of the way the propeller came in, for the two subjects are intimately connected. At its best the paddle-wheel, except for excursion steamers and certain kinds of tugs, is a very clumsy means of driving a ship through the water. It is the most obvious, because historically it is analogous to the action of the duck, of the first primitive man who paddled his small craft, or of the later Egyptians who rowed with oars down the Nile. But for open sea work the paddle-wheel is an awkward encumbrance, and apart from tugs and pleasure steamers it was last seen, in European waters at least, in the mail steamers running from England to Flushing and Ostend comparatively recently.

But for a long time there had been efforts made to introduce the screw propeller. As far back as 1804 John Stevens crossed the Hudson in a little vessel driven by a screw propeller, but it was not until thirty-two years later that John Ericsson, a Swedish engineer, reintroduced the screw and patented it. In 1837 his propeller was successfully tried in the 45-foot *Francis B. Ogden*, and in the following year the Lairds built at Birkenhead the 63-foot *Robert F. Stockton*, which obtained the extraordinary speed of thirteen knots on the Thames, going with the tide, and she afterwards went across the Atlantic, where she was turned into a tug.

But in England Francis Smith was at work on the screw problem and obtained a patent in the same year as Ericsson, and his invention was tried with success in a 6-ton boat. Smith's patent was bought by a syndicate; and in 1838 was launched the 240-ton three-master *Archimedes*, fitted with Smith's screw, and after she had steamed round Great Britain and across the Bay of Biscay, the prejudiced and "old-timers" began to believe in the new idea. Next year was launched the much larger *Novelty*, which was the first cargo ship to be fitted with a screw, and she proceeded from London to Constantinople and back. She was also the first ship to be fitted with an iron mast.

We have thus arrived at the stage when the iron ship and the screw propeller had become practicable, and thus the future of the steamer was moulded. Wood was all very well until the demand for increased tonnage arrived, but when it was proposed to construct the 3618-ton *Great Britain* there was nothing for it but to use iron. Here was a ship to be 822 feet long with 50½ feet beam, able to carry 260 passengers and 1200 tons of cargo. As no contractor could be found willing to build such a ship, the Great Western Steamship Company at Bristol constructed her themselves. She was designed by Brunei, but she turned out to be an awkward, ill-fated monstrosity.

Launched in July 1843, she was unable to enter the river until December of the following year, owing to delay in the alteration of the dock. It was originally intended to fit her with the usual paddle-wheels, but the arrival of the *Archimedes* in the port caused Brunei to modify the designs, so that his ship should be driven by a six-bladed propeller. She was a curious, six-masted craft with a bowsprit and painted ports, and in July 1845, after making a trip to London, left Liverpool with sixty passengers and 600 tons of cargo, reaching New York after a voyage of fifteen days. On the return journey her best day's steaming was 287 miles. One night during September of the following year, after leaving the Mersey, she ran ashore off the Irish coast in Dundrum Bay, where she remained for eleven months exposed to all weathers. Brunei cleverly had a wooden breakwater, loaded with stones, built round her, and she was eventually refloated and taken into Liverpool. She was now sold for a quarter of her original cost of £100,000, was turned into a full-rigged ship for the Australian trade, and eventually became a coal hulk.

But in spite of her failure this ship showed that an iron hull and a screw as propeller were a practicable combination. She was divided into five water-tight compartments, she was fitted with bilge-keels to minimise rolling, and instead of the heavy wooden bulwarks possessed by contemporary ships and inherited from the time when the Tudor ships mounted their cannon, *Great Britain* had iron rails with netting,

The *Robert F. Stockton.*

An early Cross-Channel Steamer.

so that any seas shipped could get away easily. Thus, this unfortunate vessel, in spite of her ill-luck, did introduce new ideas into the Mercantile Marine. It was in 1856 that the Cunard Company built the *Persia*, of iron. She was a 3300-ton ship, but had paddle-wheels, and then, six years later, came their *Scotia*, which was the last and finest paddle-ship ever built for the Atlantic service. She had seven water-tight compartments and a double bottom, thanks to the influence of *Great Britain*, and she lowered the record of crossing the Atlantic to just two hours under the nine days. The sailing ship as a passenger-carrier across that ocean was now definitely beaten, and the future simply consisted in the more thorough perfecting of the steamships; there was no going back now, notwithstanding the fact that in the Eastern trades the full-rigged ships were still making such wonderful passages.

The advance of engineering and science, the amount of valuable data which had been obtained during these years of steam propulsion, had already brought steamship building to be no rule-of-thumb method, but a highly technical art. About the middle of the century, John Scott Russell, for instance, made some valuable researches regarding the resistance of a ship's hull passing through the water, and in 1860 Sir Edward Harland, founder of the famous Belfast yard of Harland & Wolff, introduced steamers into the Mediterranean with a length of ten times their beam.

This novel idea was so successful that when he came to build the White Star steamships he carried out that same idea, which was yet another important influence in the evolution of the modern Atlantic liner. But even in 1852 a tremendous improvement was seen in the hull of the *Victoria*, which was built of iron to the design of Brunei & Scott Russell for the Australian Royal Mail Steam Navigation Company. She was designed to embody the wave-line theory and for a speed of ten knots, and instead of the clumsy, ponderous hulls, you find in the *Victoria* smoothness, gracefulness and sweet lines. It is therefore not altogether surprising that she won the £500 prize offered by the Colonies for the fastest voyage to Australia, her time from Gravesend to Adelaide being sixty days, including two days' delay at St. Vincent.

She was propelled by a two-bladed screw. Thus in the fewest possible years a remarkable change had come over the Mercantile Marine, and though the old diehards—those fine artists of the marlin-spike—still heartily despised every kind of steamship, yet others could see well enough that an entirely new order of things had begun owing to the

THE FAMOUS *GREAT EASTERN*. AFTER HER LAUNCHING

advance in engineering. The ship, as in regard to other creatures, had to advance with the times. The first settlement in Australia had taken place as far back as 1788, and now required better lines of communication. So, too, with the East and the great strides which North and South America were making. Pioneers, emigrants, business men were exercising a pressure which could be met only in bigger and faster ships. Thanks to the peace and prosperity of the mid-Victorian era, new ideas were emerging. Gone were the days of monopolies and worn-out rules: the last trace of mediævalism in shipping had been severed, and men were thinking out freely and unfettered the problems of transport.

It was quite a remarkable achievement that in 1853 the *Himalaya* was built at Blackwall for the P. & O. line. Here was an iron vessel of 4690 tons, which succeeded in making a record run to Gibraltar at an average speed of thirteen and a half knots. No wonder that the year after she was built she was purchased by the British Government. And then came that wonder of the world, the historic *Great Eastern*, which was the biggest ship ever built for nearly fifty years, until the White Star *Baltic* came out in 1905. The *Great Eastern* is best described as a costly freak, but she shows the marvellous courage and enterprise of the Victorian age.

It was Brunei's idea that a ship should be built so as to carry a very large number of passengers and an enormous cargo all the way to Australia without having to coal anywhere on the voyage. She was to be 679 feet 6 inches long, with 82 feet 8 inches beam, of 18,915 tons, and driven by both paddles and a screw. This five-funnelled, six-masted giantess was built by Scott Russell on the Thames. She began to be built on May 1, 1854, but she was not launched at Millwall until the last day of January 1858, the first attempt to persuade her to enter the water being unsuccessful.

As a financial speculation she was a failure. The attempts to launch her and the ensuing delay ran into thousands of pounds, and the company which owned her had to be wound up, but she was sold to a new company for £160,000. She was unfortunately now put on the Atlantic route, where she was a financial failure also; then from 1865 to 1873 she was used in laying the Atlantic submarine telegraph cables, for which she was found suitable, and finally in 1888 she was beached and then broken up. Though in a commercial sense she had never succeeded, the *Great Eastern* did prove that she was perfectly sound structurally, and never exhibited any signs of weakness in spite of her

THE GREAT EASTERN

enormous length. But she was really years before her time.

To have built this, or indeed any big ship, of wood could not have been possible. What rendered practicable the increased length of ships, able to carry high-powered engines with much space for passengers and cargo, was the invention of the rolling-mill, which had been brought about by Henry Cort, who died in 1800. Before this was introduced, the iron after leaving the furnace had to be hammered into shape. But nowadays iron and steel can be turned out into suitable plates, so that shipbuilding really consists in riveting together so many plates as to form a steel box with shaped ends. Instead of the soft sounds of the adze and caulking chisel and the wholesome smell of tar, the shipyard of today is a pandemonium of monotonous, buzzing pneumatic riveting hammers.

There is no loving selection of timbers and planking: the steel plates and girders are just there ready to be put into position. It is highly unsentimental, but inevitable that development should proceed along these lines. During the 'seventies steel had been used for shipbuilding more or less tentatively, but it was not until the Allan liner *Buenos Ayrean* that a steel ship was seen in the Atlantic.

Mild steel, because of its ductility and strength and lightness, became much more suitable than iron, and opened up another era in the story of the steamship. With the exception of yachts, lifeboats and certain fishing craft, this is now used universally for constructing hulls. In 1873 the French had employed steel in building their war- ships, and in 1881 the Cunard *Servia* came out thus constructed. She was the largest and most powerful ship then built with the exception of *Great Eastern*, her measurements being 515 feet long, 52 feet beam and 7892 tons gross. She lowered the Atlantic voyage to seven days, one hour, thirty-eight minutes.

But a most important influence on the future of the Mercantile Marine was created when the White Star Line began their competition in the Atlantic trade. Previously their flag had flown at the masthead of a fine fleet of sailing clippers. In 1867 the managing owner of the White Star Line retired, and Mr. T. H. Ismay took over control. He began by using iron for his Australian clippers instead of wood, and two years later gave an order to Harland & Wolff, Belfast, to build steamships for the Atlantic. In August 1870 was launched the first of the fleet. This was the *Oceanic*, 420 feet long, her beam being only one-tenth of her length. That proportion was a radical departure in shipbuilding, and very different from the beamy old "waggons," as the

The Oceanic

old sailing ships were sometimes called.

This *Oceanic* is really the first of the modern steamships, and contained so many new ideas as to make all the other steamships old-fashioned. For instance, she introduced the practice of having the saloon extending the entire width and placed in the middle of the ship instead of aft. The state-rooms were placed forward and abaft the saloon, instead of opening out on to it, which had been the custom derived from the sailing ships. Moreover, the introduction of glass side-lights on a much larger scale made the interior of the ship lighter and more pleasant. In fact, what with this, the revolving chairs instead of the hard seats, the oil-lamps instead of the spluttering candles, and other details of comfort, the passenger saw that he was so well looked after that the White Star became at once a popular line. Ever since that time one company has vied with another to give the Atlantic passenger the maximum amount of pleasure and luxury. How little do many of them appreciate the contrast between the crack steamships of today and of fifty or sixty years ago, when everything had to be learned by hard and costly experience!

The *Oceanic* was a 3808-ton vessel, and became the fastest steamship afloat, her four-cylinder compound engines enabling her to average fourteen and a quarter knots. The first Atlantic line to build all its steamers of iron had been the Inman Line, which from 1850 to 1892 was one of the chief competitors in that ocean. Founded by William Inman, its successful policy was to capture the emigration trade which had been carried on by the sailing ships. Their first ships had been the *City of Glasgow* and *City of Manchester*, built of iron and propelled by a single screw. They inaugurated the custom of calling at Queenstown, and began running to New York instead of Philadelphia.

The first so-called Atlantic "greyhound" was built by the Guion Line. In 1879 came their *Arizona*, which unfortunately ran at full speed into an iceberg, but her water-tight bulkhead enabled her to get into St. John's, Newfoundland. Her advent was followed by the *Oregon*, built in 1882, and she created a sensation by making the run from Queenstown to New York in six days, fourteen hours. This was a 7375-ton ship, which, with her speed of nineteen knots, made her the fastest vessel afloat, and was purchased by the Cunard Company; but she in turn was eclipsed by the two famous Cunarders, *Umbria* in 1884 and *Etruria* in the following year. These two wonderful craft were to be used as armed cruisers if required, and never were more satisfactory ships built to give their owners so little trouble. In respect of speed,

S.S. *Sultan*

also, they broke all records, *Etruria* crossing from Queenstown to New York in six days, six hours and thirty-six minutes in 1883, while seven years later *Umbria* surpassed this by maintaining an average of over nineteen and a half knots.

And whilst all this activity was proceeding in the Atlantic, ships driven by steam were running regularly to the East, though the competition in this sphere was not keen. In 1877 the Orient Line was founded. One of their ships, the *Austral*, launched in 1881, was lying in Sydney Harbour with her scuttles open, but owing to a heavy list caused through unequal coaling the water poured in and she sank in fifty feet of water. She was, however, refloated several months later.

Up till the 'eighties it was customary for the crack liners to carry three and even four masts with yards and both a fore staysail and square-sails. It was a practice which exhibited the last suspicion of steam, for it was argued that if the propeller should become damaged, or the shaft break there would at least be canvas enough for her to get along. But, with the introduction and general adoption of the twin screw, masts became fewer, yards and canvas disappeared, and the seaman who had been brought up to go aloft and lay-out along a yard found himself a mere deck hand. He had seen the golden age of the full-rigged pass away, and the last resemblance in the steamship to the Black wall frigates and the clippers remained only in the clipper bows of the Inman Line, who for so long kept up the useless but ornamental bowsprit even as late as the 'nineties. It is with the launch of their *City of New York* and *City of Paris,* the latter in 1888, that twin screws of a large size were introduced into the Mercantile Marine, and here begins the final chapter in the steamship's development, for it gave her an independence and increase of efficiency which never before has she possessed nor since lost.

S.S. Orient

Chapter 16

The Modern Merchant Ship

The dominating factors which now influenced the development of the Atlantic liner were speed and comfort. Owing to the rapid increase of commerce between the United States and Great Britain, the West had long since taken the place of the Orient as a magnetic attraction for the ship-owner. It is the Atlantic and not the route to India which has seen the great improvements in the modern ship, and even if there had been keener competition to the East, it would not have been possible to increase much the size of steamships for the reason of the limitations imposed by the Suez Canal. It is conceivable, however, that someday the route to Australia round the Cape may become a lane of keen rivalry to the advantage of ship development.

The struggle for the speed supremacy of the North Atlantic went on. The *City of Paris* was a flier. She could do her nineteen and twenty knots. But the White Star Line replied with the *Teutonic* and *Majestic*, both launched in 1889. They, too, were fliers, for the former broke the record by steaming from Queenstown to New York in five days, eighteen hours, eight minutes, while the latter did it in five days, sixteen hours, thirty-one minutes. They were, of course, twin-screw ships, but of only 9984 tons, which in this advanced twentieth century seems quite small for a crack liner.

The competition was continued by the Cunard Company launching in 1892 the Campania, and in the following year the *Lucania*, fitted with twin screws and triple-expansion engines. Beautiful ships these were, with lovely lines and an amazing turn of speed. Steel had, of course, long since taken the place of iron, and in the building of these two wonderful vessels the plates were made of unprecedented size, and so they required a smaller number of rivets. These were 600-feet ships, and it was their length which helped to give them the 22-knot

S.S. Spain

speed. *Campania* made the run between Queenstown and New York in five and a half days, and averaged just under twenty-two knots for a whole year's east-bound voyages. This was a truly remarkable performance for the real criterion of efficiency is that a ship should be able not merely to make one spectacular hours run, nor break the record for one day or one voyage, but to keep on doing this all the time. Here is the test of good steamship management ashore, perfect organisation aboard and the reason for the highest praise to her officers and crew

The point we have now reached represents the era of keen competition for the best-equipped and speediest steamships in the Atlantic, and therefore of all the Mercantile Marines in the world In this race the Collins Line, though subsidised by the American Government, had already disappeared the reorganised Inman Line, which had been absorbed in the American Line in spite of in the its fine ships, ceased to be a dangerous competitor In the end it became a contest between the two British lines, the Cunard and the White Star. The German liners now entered the Atlantic as very serious competitors. It will be more convenient to deal with the German Mercantile Marine in a separate chapter, but it may be said here that it was the wonderful achievements of *Campania* and *Lucania* which created such emulation that the North German Lloyd Company scrapped their old-fashioned ships and in 1897 produced the *Kaiser Wilhelm der Grosse*, which by her mean speed of 22.81 knots beat the Cunarders, and thus for the first time Germany won the "blue riband" of the Atlantic, as the expression was in the 'nineties.

In 1899 came the British reply in size though not in speed. This was the White Star *Oceanic*, 13 feet longer than the memorable *Great Eastern*, measuring 705 feet, as against the German's 648 feet 7 inches. *Oceanic's* 28,500 tons displacement showed the extraordinary development which had taken place in the shipbuilding art in the fewest years, and she was able to maintain a speed of twenty knots. The Cunard's next ships were two, *Ivernia* and *Saxonia*, each of about 14,000 tons gross—that is to say, roughly the size of the German champion, but with an average speed of fifteen and a quarter knots. They were comfortable and economical rather than record-breakers. But the *Ivernia* was the first Atlantic liner to break away from the triple-expansion and use the quadruple-expansion system. The White Star Line, in 1901 and 1903, respectively, brought out two enormous but slow ships in the *Celtic* and *Cedric*, the former being 20,880 tons and the latter

THE *BRITANNIC*

THE *CAMPANIA*

21,034 tons, with an average speed of sixteen knots, and at this time also came their 15,801-ton *Arabic*, with the same speed.

There was therefore a kind of lull in British enterprise, and in 1903 the Germans caused another sensation by the *Kaiser Wilhelm the Second*, which was able to do her twenty-three and a half knots as an average speed from New York to Plymouth. But a new development was again to take place. Competition was so keen in the steamship world, there was such an impetus to the builder, and so many clever minds were working on the problems of propulsion, that it was inevitable that all these wonderful changes should come about in such rapid succession. In the year 1886 the triple-expansion engine had come into general use. This had been followed by the quadruple-expansion, as already mentioned, and now came a still further change.

For some time the turbine engine had been employed for driving electric dynamos on land, for pumping stations, colliery fans and so on. But in 1894 this type was installed experimentally in the 44-ton craft called the *Turbinia*, which was seen racing along Spithead at thirty-four knots. It was a wonderful sight, but it was not until 1905 that this type of engine was introduced into merchant ships, when the Atlantic ships *Virginian* [1] and *Victorian* of the Allan Line were fitted with Parsons' triplicate turbines driving three propellers. In the same year the Cunard produced their first turbine liner, *Carmania*, which on her trial attained a speed of twenty knots. She was built of a strength in excess of Board of Trade requirements, no fewer than 1,800,000 rivets being used in her construction, each plate being thirty-two feet long. But for the excellence of her construction she would never have been able to emerge successfully from her famous duel when she sank the Cap Trafalgar off the South American coast during the first autumn of the recent Great War.

Events happen so quickly, and one sensation follows so rapidly on another, that we are apt sometimes to get quite a wrong perspective. To me the *Carmania* is one of the most interesting ships afloat. For nine years before the war she did most excellent work as one of the finest passenger ships, carrying many thousands of people across the Atlantic in comfort and luxury. Then came the war, and *Carmania* became an armed merchant cruiser and was sent into South American waters. She met the Hamburg-South America liner *Cap Trafalgar*, a very similar ship, also armed as a merchant cruiser, off the island of Trinidada,

---

1 Now owned by the Swedish-American Line and named the *Drottningholm*.

and then fought a terrific duel which lasted eighty minutes, during which the Cunarder was pierced by seventy-nine shells, set seriously on fire and generally made desolate. But she sank the *Cap Trafalgar*, and today, and since the war, *Carmania* has resumed carrying her thousands across to New York in perfect luxury again, with veranda cafés, costly furniture, palm trees and the rest, just as if nothing serious had ever happened. Truly the modern ship is an amazing creature.

During the war 56 *per cent*, of the Cunard ships were sunk, including the memorable *Lusitania*; and the White Star Line, owing to the same reason, lost close on 150,000 tons. The *Mauretania* and *Lusitania* had followed the *Carmania*, and were the outcome of an agreement made with the British Government to produce two ships capable of maintaining a minimum average ocean speed of from twenty-four to twenty-five knots in moderate weather. This has not only been maintained, but surpassed. *Mauretania* was built in 1907, with turbines, a length of 790 feet, and her tonnage is 31,000 gross. In spite of all her running before the war, during the war, and since, she still holds the record not merely for the Atlantic, but for all seas in respect of merchant ships.

The test accepted by most shipping experts is two-fold: the highest average speed for the whole voyage, and the fastest passage in days, hours and minutes. On this reckoning *Mauretania* still leads, in spite of her younger sisters, for as recently as 1922 she averaged 25.29 knots eastward-bound in June. Her fastest passage in July of that year of five days, eight hours, nine minutes, entitles her still more to possession of the "blue riband" of the Atlantic. But as showing the remarkable consistency in running, if we take her three consecutive passages eastward across the Atlantic in June and July 1922, there are only five minutes difference between the fastest and the slowest. It is superfluous to comment on this achievement

At a time when her fighting sister *Indomitable* is being broken up, this powerful merchantman still goes on beating records. Recently fitted to burn oil-fuel, this turbine-driven, quadruple-screw, twenty-five knotter will long be remembered in maritime history as *Lusitania* will in naval history. [2]

---

2. The speeds given for *Mauretania, Majestic, Berengaria, Aquitania, Olympic* and *Homeric* are from New York to Cherbourg Breakwater or to the Eddystone Light. The passages quoted are really not faster than what was previously accomplished on the Liverpool to New York route before these big liners were transferred to the Southampton to New York route. (Continued next page.)

BERTHING A BIG LINER

The next famous Atlantic ships were the two White Star liners *Titanic* and *Olympic*. The tragic end of the former, when she foundered during her maiden voyage, is too well remembered to need relating again. The *Olympic* left Southampton on her maiden voyage in June 1911. She is a triple-screw vessel of 46,439 tons gross register, and thus much bigger than *Mauretania*, but not quite so fast. Those of us who remember passing *Olympic* at sea during the war, zigzagging through the submarine zone with 5000 soldiers on board and the ship's boats swung out, will never forget the sight.

One hears many impossible yarns about certain claims, but apart from her magnificent work in bringing armies from America to Europe safely, this ship did definitely sink a German submarine. This may be regarded as some compensation for the loss of that new triple-screw White Star *Britannic*, a vessel of 48,158 tons gross register, which was destined never to cross the Atlantic, for which she had been constructed. The reader will remember that on November 21, 1916, after much excellent service as a hospital ship, she was sunk by enemy action in the Zea Channel, Ægean Sea.

Olympic came out as the world's biggest ship, and she is one of the fastest. On one occasion coming up Channel she recently touched 27.82 knots for a brief spell, but her best average speed for a whole voyage is 22.55 knots, and her quickest passage is five days, nineteen hours, twelve minutes. For the consideration of the big German liners who were competing with these efforts the reader is referred to the chapter dealing with the rise and fall of the German Mercantile Marine, but the next British mammoth was the *Aquitania*, which was put into the Cunard service just before the war began. She is over 900 feet long, she can steam at a little more than twenty-three knots, and her best passage, east-bound, has been five days, nineteen hours, forty-one minutes. Her gross tonnage is 47,000.

I watched *Aquitania* being built, from the time when she was a mere mass of steel, and finally saw her take the water in the Clyde, and walked all over her half an hour before this impressive event took place. She was barely ready for her intended work than she was turned

---

Thus the fastest Atlantic voyage ever made was by *Mauretania* when she steamed from Queenstown to New York in four days, ten hours, forty-one minutes. *Lusitania* accomplished this in only sixty-one minutes longer. The best average speed ever made by a liner for one day was 27'10 knots by *Lusitania*, eastward bound; but the best average speed for a whole voyage was made by *Mauretania*, before being converted to oil. She kept up 26 06 knots

Modern Navigation

into an armed merchant cruiser and joined Admiral Phipps Hornby's Cruiser Squadron on the Atlantic trade route. But it was rather like putting a race-horse to do the work of a cart-horse. *Aquitania* was then, like other merchantmen, coal-burning, and her endurance was only six days, for she was built for the purpose of rushing across the Atlantic, then filling up and returning as fast as she could. She was thus not suitable for patrolling, and after colliding with a Leyland liner, whilst under the command of a naval officer, *Aquitania* terminated her engagement as a warship, and then did far more useful work during the time of hostilities, until she again took up her peaceable service.

This was the last British-built merchant ship to be constructed of mammoth size that is still afloat. The White Star *Homeric*, which joined the Atlantic service in the spring of 1922, is an ex-German vessel. This ship is neither as big nor as fast as *Aquitania*, but she is the largest twin-screw steamer afloat. Her best average speed for a whole trip is 18.69 knots, and her best voyage is six days, nineteen hours, twenty-two minutes. But the slump which followed the war and the depression which came over the shipping trade made it undesirable to lay down any more of these leviathans for the present, and there was still another reason.

In Germany were two such vessels, one of which was already built and had been running for a year or two, and the other, a still bigger ship, was not yet finished. These two ships were handed over to Great Britain, the former being the *Imperator*, 52,022 tons, launched in 1912, which used to call at Southampton on her way from Germany to New York. The other ship was the 56,551-ton *Bismarck*, whose keel had been laid by the Kaiser in the year 1914. The *Vaterland*, as mentioned in another chapter, measuring 950 feet and 52,282 tons, was acquired by the United States. The *Imperator* now became the *Berengaria*, and was taken over by the Cunard Company; the *Bismarck* became the *Majestic*, and was put into the White Star service in the spring of 1922. She was built at the Blohm and Voss yard, Hamburg, and with her enormous tonnage and length of 956 feet is the biggest ship in the world.

Though built in Germany, which learned the art from Great Britain, these two ships are now the pride of the British Merchant Fleet, and they are, together with the *Mauretania* and *Aquitania*, consumers not of coal, but of oil. The *Berengaria* measures 919 feet long, is practically 100 feet in beam, and represents an enormous amount of capital; but she was laid aside for six or seven months so as to have a complete overhaul and to be converted from coal-burning. With that fuel she had been able to do a little over twenty-three knots, and her best average speed has since been 23.88 knots for the whole voyage; her fastest trip being five days, eighteen hours, forty-seven minutes.

You can imagine the responsibility of her captain, handling such an enormous steel island. Let us forget for a moment such things as her new ballroom, able to accommodate 250 dancers. Let us forget, too, the cafes, gymnasia, palm courts, Turkish and swimming-baths and the numbers of private suites, the velvet carpets, and baronial halls; let us just think of her as a ship.

Eighty-five feet above the water is the sun-deck promenade, and away above that again rises the bridge. Here are all sorts of gadgets, such as a bell that rings automatically when the temperature of the sea drops below a certain degree, and so the warning is made to the officer of the watch that icebergs are about. Tell-tale lamps act as fire-indicators, and another bell rings to call attention to the fact that there is smoke in some section of the ship. Steam pressure is then made to drive water down a pipe to spray around the particular compartment. There are telephones galore, from the bridge to the engine-room, boiler-rooms, baggage-hold, purser's office, engineer's office and, *via* the ship's central exchange, to all parts of the ship.

Berengaria, like *Vaterland*, had a good deal of trouble with her water-tube boilers, which were similar to the German naval pattern, but in *Majestic* British engineers introduced some modifications whilst she was still being completed at Hamburg. The point is this. Whereas these water-tube boilers are all right for a man-of-war, which normally steams at fifteen knots and only occasionally is whacked up to twenty-one and above, the liner is driven hard all the time, and has to maintain her full speed day and night until she gets across the ocean. The amount of oil-fuel required for *Berengaria* to cross the Atlantic once is about 6000 tons, and this is carried in side or wing-bunkers. A hundred tons an hour can be supplied to each of the four boiler-rooms, and the engines are, of course, turbines.

It is said that £1,000,000 was the price the White Star Line paid for the *Majestic*, and she was a great bargain at that, for she would cost four times that amount to be built today. There are forty-eight boilers, and she can carry enough oil-fuel for the round voyage Southampton-New York-Southampton. This means not merely greater efficiency in regard to steaming, but saves time and expense in bunkering and cleaning ship, for it takes only six hours and very few men to

THE *BERENGARIA*

get the 7000 tons on board. Her best average speed in a passage is over twenty-four knots, and her quickest voyage five days, nine hours, forty-two minutes. When she was handed over to the Reparations Commission under the terms of the Peace Treaty her speed was returned as twenty-three knots. But the White Star officials were not a little surprised to find, while bringing the ship to Southampton from Hamburg, that her turbines would develop much more power than they were credited with, and that she was really a 25-knot ship. In fact, on one occasion she did an average of twenty-seven knots for over five hours eastward-bound.

It is significant that more than half the length of the ship is taken up with the propelling machinery. Never were such large machinery and boiler plant installed in one vessel. If you think of an eight-roomed house and multiply this by 400, you get some idea of her interior space. She is practically a floating town, with its smart hotel, suites, clubs, and so on located on her nine steel decks; and four propellers to keep this town hurrying across the Atlantic. Swimming-bath, two royal suites, 1245 state-rooms, a restaurant, palm court, foyer, lounge-there is no end to her luxurious internal arrangement.

And yet there are all sorts of cunning devices to ensure safety. To guard against fire, the steel bulkheads have been coated with fireproof material; the main staircases are so arranged that they can be isolated and thus ensure a means of escape to the upper decks. There are 450 fire alarms distributed throughout the ship, which indicate automatically to the officer on the bridge.

There are three wireless stations. The largest enables her to maintain permanent connection with both the Old and the New World during the whole voyage. The second is for use over a distance of 800 miles, and the third is for emergency. There are anti-rolling tanks, submarine signalling gear, and indeed every ingenious device that the wit of man could invent for the safety and welfare of the 4000 passengers she takes care of each trip. During Cowes week 1922 King George V paid to her, and through her to the British Mercantile Marine, a singular honour in going aboard to inspect her. His Royal Standard was broken out at the main, and this is one of the very few occasions during the last four hundred years when a merchant ship, serving as such, has legally hoisted this flag.

It did occur in the year 1913, when His Majesty inspected the *Mauretania* at Liverpool; and on that day a Harbour Board tug while taking the King to and from the liner flew the Royal Ensign. But prior

S.S. *Olympic*

S.S. *Majestic*

to that I think we have to go right back to the year 1495, when Henry VII granted to John Cabot and his sons the right to fly the royal banners and flags during their voyages of discovery.

From the *Majestic* to the earliest merchantmen of the Mediterranean, even looking back a hundred years to the time when the old East Indiamen of 1000 tons were wallowing along, or the Falmouth packets were braving the Atlantic, seems to us a period of time that is hardly believable. In spite of wars and every kind of crises, never has the merchant ship so utterly and marvellously transformed herself within such a few years. It is a triumph of man over matter that he can build up such a creation as a 50,000-ton ship, but there are just two things which always seem to me more wonderful still. The first is that you can ever launch such a mass of steel safely from the land down the ways into the water; and the second is that, having fitted her out for sea, she can be made obedient to the mind of her commander-checked, spurred on, controlled and moved about across the sea at will, with confidence and remarkable regularity.

It is an interesting experience to control finance, it is a great task to control men, and it is a responsible task to control the ship of State. But to control the biggest ship in the history of the world, costing over £1,000,000 sterling and containing several thousands of travellers, from quay to quay, through any kind of weather that may come along—this to me seems, above all, a full-sized man's job. It is one that brings forth everything that is best and noble in the calling of a sailor—courage, coolness, organising ability, leadership, self-reliance, dependability, tact, discipline.

Below are the saloons, orchestra, dancing, laughter, luxury and thousands of brilliant lights. On the bridge the silent darkness of a black, starless night; just the glimmer from the bowls of the gyro-compass repeaters, the quartermaster at the wheel, a couple of messengers standing by, and the officer of the watch. And always the wild roar of the wind as the ship tears on her way at twenty odd knots; while forward is the swish of the sea as the fine bows throw each bursting wave aside. It is a study in contrasts, just that immeasurable gulf which has always existed between the life of the landsman and the sailor from the earliest days of history until the present day. To the former "the wonder is always new that any sane man can be a sailor," as Emerson put it. But it was the same philosopher who admitted that " the sea is masculine, the type of active strength."

And, happily, there is such a contagion as sea-fever. Without it there

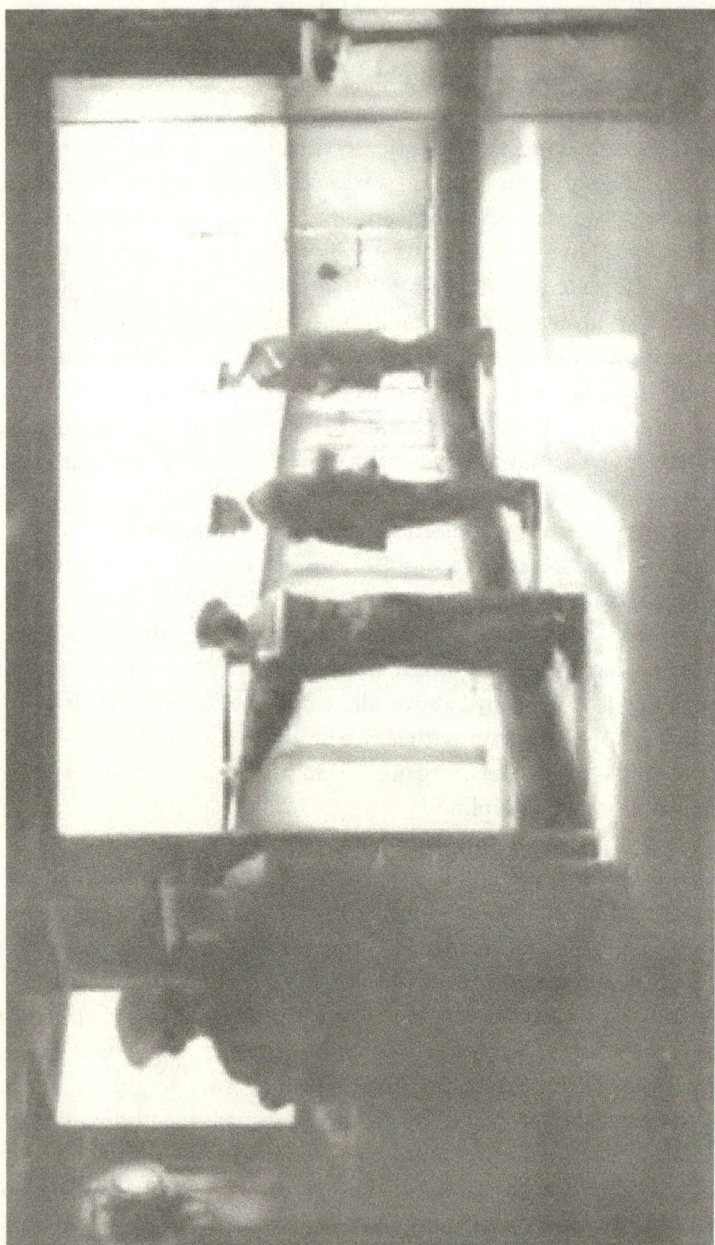

THE BRIDGE OF THE WORLD'S BIGGEST SHIP

would have been no Phoenician, Venetian, Spanish, Portuguese, Norse, mediaeval or later mariners; no new worlds to discover—nothing but a very restricted communication and the minimum of progress. It would have been a very stunted, dull existence. There would have been no fine merchantmen of the sea and none of that glorious breed of seamen, virile, strong and masculine. Let us be thankful for all that the sea has taught us.

CHAPTER 17

The Rise and Fall of the German Mercantile Marine

For about seventy years the German Mercantile Marine had an interesting career. It began in quite a small way, it was conducted with courage, enterprise, far-sightedness and, eventually, with an astute cunning which many people would describe under a stronger term. Its rise was meteoric, and its descent at the time of its zenith was swifter still. It is just because the true value of the sea began to be appreciated, that Germany was able to build up such a vast and highly efficient service within one generation. The result was that on the eve of the Great War she was second only to the British Empire as a big owner of steamships.

At that date 60 *per cent*, of Germany's shipping was in the hands of ten lines, working together with a solidarity that amounted practically to a shipping union. These ten were the Hamburg-America Line, the North German Lloyd, the Hamburg South-American Line, the Hansa Line, the German Australian Line, the Kosmos Line, the Roland Line, the German East Africa Line, the Woermann Line and the Hamburg-Bremen-Africa Line. A month before the outbreak of war this huge organisation comprised 3,194,000 gross tons, to say nothing of the German Levant Line of 155,000 tons. Well organised, reaching to every part of the world, subsidised by the German Government to the extent of £107,950 a year, this association was extremely successful in obtaining an enormous amount of the world's carrying trade and in furthering Germany's political aspirations.

It was able to put up the severest competition and to draw away from the United Kingdom a good deal of carrying trade, and in their fight with the British companies of steamships the Germans were

BIG SHIP MASTERS

helped not merely by subsidies, but by attractive through-rates over their railway system. It was their unity and energy in organisation, their ability to cut rates, and their attention to the smallest details which gave them their vast success.

It is important to emphasise one great distinction. The British Isles depend for their supplies and overseas trade on the tramp steamer. Of the British tonnage before the war 60 *per cent*, represented tramp tonnage and only 40 per cent, liners, and it was essential for the nation to have a large amount of "loose" tonnage able to trade at short notice to any part of the world, taking out, for instance, cheap coal and coming back with cargoes of grain, cotton, wool, rice and so on. This policy was the exact opposite of Germany, which built up its Mercantile Marine on liner trades, and especially in the Atlantic, their interest in tramp steamers being quite small. Now of those ten German lines just mentioned the Hamburg-America and the North German Lloyd, owning on the eve of war 1,093,000 and 716,000 gross tons respectively, were at once the creative forces and the mainstays of German shipping. Therefore if we consider their history we have before us practically the whole evolution of the German Mercantile Marine.

The Hamburg-America Line at the time war broke out was the largest merchant steamship enterprise in the world, owning between 400 and 500 ships, with seventy-five distinct services, its vessels calling at 400 of the leadings ports of the world and carrying over 400,000 passengers a year. It was thus an enormous corporation, that makes the old Honourable East India Company look ridiculous. As a means of providing national wealth and the ready transportation of German goods into the remotest corners of the globe it was invaluable. It was founded on May 27, 1847, with a capital of 465,000 *marks*, and it ordered three sailing ships in England of about 717 tons each, which carried a score of first-class passengers and a couple of hundred emigrants and a little freight. These were full-rigged, three-masted vessels, with heavy quarters, the white riband and painted square ports and the high-steeved bowsprit so familiar in English shipping. The average trip from Hamburg to New York took forty days, and twenty-nine days on the return voyage. These three ships were the *Deutschlandy, Nordamerika* and *Rhein*.

In 1854 the company had already prospered so much, thanks largely to the emigrant traffic, that it decided to go in for steam. The screw was replacing the paddle in British ships and iron was being used instead of wood. They therefore gave an order to Caird of Greenock to build a couple of 2026-ton screw steamers having a speed of about twelve knots. The first of these was the *Borussia*, a three-masted vessel with sails, clipper bow and one funnel. She made her appearance in 1856. Hitherto British and other seamen had been largely employed for crews, but now only Germans, dressed in uniform, and disciplined after the custom of a man-of-war, were allowed. The German Mercantile Marine was beginning to exist by itself.

The best speed obtained with these ships was sixteen days, and in 1858 came the *Saxonia* and *Austria*, which reduced the passage eastward-bound to a little over twelve days, the firm's fleet now consisting of eight sailing ships and four steamers. Presently the former were all sold, and a fortnightly service to New York was instituted, and other steamships were added. At the outbreak of the American Civil War this line was carrying the United States mails and calling at Southampton, and, after leaving the English port, New York was reached in ten days. By the early 'seventies the fleet already numbered twenty-five steamships, and was also running to the Spanish Main, Mexico and West Indies.

The White Star and the Hamburg-America were the first Atlantic lines to adopt the twin-screw system for passenger ships. It was in 1887 that the latter ordered the two steel, twin-screw ships *Columbia* and *Auguste Victoria*. The former was built at Birkenhead by Lairds, but the latter was constructed at Stettin, and this was the first time a German yard had attempted a ship of such a size, for she measured over 500 feet long, and she was of 8430 tons burthen. These two vessels were immediately followed by two others, similar in type, of which one was built on the Clyde and one at Stettin. With their three funnels, high speed, improved ventilation, commodious cabins, bathrooms, suites of rooms and general high standard of comfort, this quartette made a sensation. It was the introduction of the German floating palaces into the Atlantic.

Reference to the previous two chapters in this volume will show that the British Atlantic companies were meeting this competition, but if you ask now was it that, notwithstanding the fact that the German Empire had been proclaimed as recently as 1871, this new Mercantile Marine had been able to build up such a trade in so few years, the answer is this. The repeal of the British Navigation Laws in 1849 enabled the Prussian ships to have the opportunity which came at the right moment. But, secondly, it was the enormous increase of emigrant passengers anxious to leave the European continent and try their fortunes in the New World. I have no wish to weary the reader with statistics, but the following few figures will substantiate this argument. They are derived from a Board of Trade analysis based on information afforded by the United States Immigration Bureau, and are therefore beyond dispute.

Bearing in mind that the first Hamburg-America ship sailed in 1847, we find that whereas the average annual emigration from Germany to the U.S.A. had been only 19,000 up to 1844, during the next ten years it jumped to 95,000, dropped during the next decade to 49,000, but then rose to 113,000 in the decennial period ending 1874, was 109,000 up to the year 1884, then dropped to 28,000 by 1904, but rose to 34,000 in the decade ending 1914. But in addition to these figures must be added others. By reason of her geographical position Germany was most favourably placed for capturing the emigrant traffic from the rest of the continent, and of this she made the best advantage. It was not until the decade ending 1874 that the Russians, for instance, began pouring out from their own country to North America, and gradually the German ships carried most of these. How valuable such a traffic was can be at once realised. Beginning with an average of 2000 Russian emigrants to the United States, this figure in ten years had increased to 10,000, then to 88,000 and, finally, just before the war averaged 199,000.

In 1894 the German Government erected what were known as control stations at various places on the Russian frontier, ostensibly to prevent the spread of cholera by Russian emigrants travelling through Germany. The erection and management of these controls were vested in the Hamburg-America and North German Lloyd Lines. But whatever was their original purpose, these stations came to be used by the German steamship companies for confining the increasing stream of emigrants to their own lines, who made it as difficult as possible for persons not travelling by those lines to get through the control stations. In addition to this, the German Government so legislated as to make it very awkward and more costly for emigrants to get to America in British ships. Thus, Germany, by doing everything from intimidation and bluff to legislation, did succeed in obtaining a most valuable emigrant traffic, and so was able, quite apart from her own increasing exports, to build up a thoroughly up-to-date and steadily improving Merchant Navy.

It is not to be wondered at that now she had learnt to construct steel steamships for herself she made a bold bid for Atlantic merchant-ship supremacy. By the year of the Paris Exhibition in 1900 this line had fourteen twin-screw steamers to carry passengers across. The latest was the celebrated *Deutschland*, which was to win the "blue riband" of the Atlantic; for this record-smasher succeeded in lowering the voyage between New York and Plymouth to five days, seven hours, thirty-eight minutes, and on one trip averaged 23.51 knots. This four-funnelled ship was of 16,502 tons and measured 686 feet long. She was certainly an eye-pleasing vessel, for it was before the practice of building lofty superstructures had become the fashion. Her biggest day's run was 601 knots, and the sumptuousness of her passenger comfort made her a very popular ship. In 1906 came the *Kaiserin Auguste Victoria*, 24,581 tons, 687 feet long, and able to carry 4000 passengers and crew. She was at the time the biggest steamer in the world.

But before we mention the mammoth German liners we must see briefly how the North German Lloyd grew up. Their first transatlantic steamer was the *Bremen*, built by Caird of Greenock in 1858, but their real progress commences with the year 1881, when the first German "express" steamer entered the line. This was the 4510-ton *Elbe*, a four-masted screw ship built on the Clyde, and during the next ten years Glasgow built *Ems* and seven other British-made vessels, whose speed varied from sixteen to eighteen knots. They were able to carry 1200 passengers. But when we come to the 'nineties the passenger trade was so good that the North German Lloyd could afford to scrap its old-fashioned craft and build the twin-screw *Kaiser Wilhelm der Grosse*. This was to become an historic ship.

She measured 14,349 gross tons, and appeared in 1897. The Germans were jealous of the achievements which had been made by the Cunard *Campania* and *Lucania*, and by attaining a mean speed of 22.81 knots on her trip from New York to Europe did outstrip the Cunarders' fine record; and thus for the first time the "blue riband" of the Atlantic temporarily passed to Germany. She was "made in Germany"—at Stettin—and this triumphant voyage did a great deal to encourage the German Mercantile Marine and German shipbuilders. She had been constructed on the understanding that if during the trial trip across the Atlantic she did not come up to the requirements of the contract, the North German Lloyd were to be allowed to reject her. Actually she surpassed the builders' undertaking.

In 1907, whilst coming across the Atlantic in October weather eastward-bound, this handsome ship fractured her rudder; but instead of taking her into Halifax, the nearest port, her captain held on for

Plymouth and thence to Bremerhaven, the ship having been manoeuvred by means of her twin screws. It was a fine achievement, but some ships are born to be adventurous. At the beginning of the Great War the *Kaiser Wilhelm der Grosse* was in Germany. She was fitted out as a raider, left Hamburg on August 4, 1914, evaded the Grand Fleet, passed round the north of Iceland, and on August 7 sank a British trawler, then proceeded down the Atlantic, sank a couple and molested two more ships, and finally went into the Rio de Oro, a lonely anchorage in Spanish territory in North-West Africa. But on August 26 arrived H.M.S. *Highflyer,* and as the German refused to leave territorial waters, the British cruiser opened fire and destroyed her. Thus, after nearly twenty years' service, this former Atlantic greyhound ended her days as an armed merchant cruiser.

The North German Lloyd's *Kaiser Wilhelm II* was the next ship of this line to cause a sensation. This was in 1903, and she was certainly a triumph for the Stettin builders. Of 20,000 registered tons, she was a little faster even than the *Kaiser Wilhelm der Grosse,* for she kept up an average speed of 23.58 knots between New York and Plymouth in one voyage. Very useful was this speed to become eleven years later, for she was in the North Atlantic when war broke out, and got safely into New York on August 6.

The *George Washington*, of 26,000 gross register tons, was launched as the biggest of all the ships in the German Mercantile Marine, though, with the speed of eighteen and a half knots, by no means the fastest. She was added to the N.D.L. in 1908, and was able to carry just under 8000 passengers for her owners when the list was full. A very useful and luxurious ship she turned out to be, but on the day after the war began she arrived in New York, was interned, and is now one of the ships in the American Mercantile Marine. The *Berlin,* another N.D.L. steamer, passed into the owners' hands in 1909. She was of 19,200 gross tons, and originally could do her eighteen knots. In the autumn of 1914 she laid the big minefield off the north coast of Ireland, on which H.M.S. *Audacious* and other ships foundered. Berlin afterwards scurried north and interned herself in Norway.

Such, then, was the progress of these two main supports of the German Mercantile Marine until the coming of the mammoth Atlantic liners. The ships of the Hamburg-America and the North German Lloyd were admittedly as good, and sometimes better than, their competitors, the Cunard and White Star; and during the period immediately preceding the war, competition was very keen not merely on the

New York route, but in the trade with Central America, South America, East Africa and Australia. The German Mercantile Marine was everywhere, and cutting rates in an alarming manner. Her sea-borne trade was increasing, but the bulk of her shipping still remained, on the eve of war, in the ten powerful companies; and her main strength was still in the Atlantic trade of the two big lines we have just been considering.

The North Atlantic had long since earned the title of the cockpit where the mercantile supremacy at sea was to be fought out. Germany's final bid was a great effort. For in the year 1912 was built the 23½-knot *Imperator*, a stupendous creature of 52,022 tons, with her swimming-bath and super-luxury. In 1914 was put into service the 26.75-knot *Vaterland*, which was bigger still, for she measured 950 feet long, against *Imperator's* 905 feet, and her tonnage worked out at 52,282. The former at the outbreak of war was lucky to be in Germany, where she remained until after hostilities. She was handed over to the Cunard Company, who changed her name to *Berengaria*. The *Vaterland* got into New York on the day war was declared between Great Britain and Germany, and was interned. She was eventually used for carrying American troops to Europe, and after the war she passed into the American Mercantile Marine, who changed her name to *Leviathan*.

When she was seized from Germany there were no plans of her available. The United States Shipping Board, on making inquiries from her German builders as to the price of these plans, were asked the enormous sum of $1,000,000. This was declined, and the colossal task of preparing these plans from the ship herself was successfully undertaken. But you may imagine what it means to run a ship of this size when it cost the American Mercantile Marine $50,000 a month merely to keep her efficient whilst laid up. Finally there was finished in Germany during 1922 the third mammoth, of 56,000 tons. Originally intended to be called the *Bismarck*, she was handed over to the White Star Line, who changed her name to *Majestic*.

Before the war Germany's Mercantile Marine, according to the Managing Director of the Hamburg-America Line, consisted of 5,459,000 gross tons. Of this amount approximately she lost owing to war operations 2,700,000 tons. By reason of the Treaty of Versailles she lost a further 2,900,000 tons approximately, leaving her about 400,000 tons. [1] If we select the spring of 1922 we are neither too near the

1. That is, tonnage built during the war.

STOKEHOLD

STARTING PLATFORM

ending of the war nor too far removed from it to notice the efforts which are being made to revive a merchant fleet which so suddenly vanished from its high position. The Hamburg-America Line in 1922 had but forty-three vessels of 165,707 gross tons, and the North German Lloyd only twenty-five ships of 127,098 gross tons. A mighty contrast to the summer of 1914. But both these and other lines were going ahead with their building, and it was unofficially estimated that the German Merchant Fleet on May 31, 1922, consisted of 1,546,000 gross tons.

In accordance with the Peace Treaty all German merchant ships of any importance were handed over to the Entente Powers. This, in part, was as compensation for the loss of tonnage during the U-boat campaign. But Germany recompensed her shipping companies for the merchant vessels thus surrendered and gave them every encouragement to build up once more the fleets which meant so much to her, financially and politically. For the Shipping Redemption Agreement of 1921 indemnified these companies, provided labour for the shipyards, and ensured co-operation of the industries inland. The money paid to the companies was taken from the national funds, but its distribution and the supervision of the building programme have been entrusted to a Ship-owners' Trust Company. Thus Germany still realises all that a Mercantile Marine means to her, and she has every intention of building it up again during the coming years.

CHAPTER 18

The American Mercantile Marine

Throughout the course of this story the reader will have observed many references to the American Mercantile Marine. Let us now consider how it began, developed, waned and again revived. We have seen how the enterprise of the New England builders was to have a profound effect on British shipping, but we desire now to regard the subject as a whole.

So long as a country, wherever situated, has a seaboard, it is very evident that its civilised community will soon begin building craft of some kind. The early colonists in America built a 30-ton vessel as far back as 1607, and it is from this *Virginia* that we must trace the American Mercantile Marine. Seven years later a small ship was launched at New Amsterdam, as, of course. New York was then called, and by the second decade of the seventeenth century there were over 1000 ships in colonial waters; for numbers of shipwrights had come over from England. During the eighteenth century at Portland, Maine, and elsewhere were built square-rigged ships, privateers, and the first schooners as well as brigantines. This was quite apart from the shipping and timber sent to England, and during the year 1769 the twelve colonies launched 389 ships, representing 20,000 tons.

In few countries of the world has the relation between war and mercantile shipping been so accurately reflected, as we shall see as we go on. The immediate result of the American revolution was to throttle the Atlantic trade, and five of the first eleven Acts of Congress were laws to encourage American shipping. In 1789 the State gave special privileges to shippers engaged in the East Indian and China trades. Many of these shippers and owners were located in Massachusetts, and made fine profits, as, for instance, the *Mount Vernon* of Salem, which in 1799 made a profit of $100,000 in a single round trip to China; and one ship made 700 *per cent*, on a cargo of pepper from Sumatra.

The registered American tonnage in the foreign trade grew from 123,893 tons in 1789 to 667,107 tons in 1800; for during the wars growing out of the French Revolution the American Mercantile Marine actually became the principal carriers of Europe, as at one time the Dutch and the English had been. Thus for a second time the marine showed how sensitive it was to the effect of war. But the war of 1812 caused severe losses to American merchant ships, yet, on the other hand, American privateers played havoc with English shipping. The effect, even in those days of comparatively few ships, is at once seen by looking at the port of Liverpool, the natural haven for American ships arriving in Europe; for whereas in 1810, 6729 ships entered that port, only 4599 came in during the year 1812. On the other hand, as soon as peace returned these figures jumped up, and from 1815 to 1860 shipping went ahead quickly.

For the United States were fast developing their industries, opening up trade, and therefore had every need of a Mercantile Marine. The legislation of Congress in 1828 opened up American ports to cargo-carrying British ships from any country where American vessels were on a similar footing to British ships, and two years later the West Indies were opened to American shipping. In 1849 Great Britain adopted the Free Trade policy, and full reciprocity was established between British and American merchant vessels. The history of the clipper ships and the competition between Great Britain and the United States for the ocean-carrying trade has already been related in this volume. It is only necessary once more to emphasise that war had yet again a good deal to do with the future of the American Mercantile Marine, for the Civil War of 1861 took away any chance which remained to American ships of continuing as the great sea-carriers.

The American mind had to concentrate on fighting. Meanwhile, much of the tonnage had passed under other flags, while in Great Britain the accessibility of coal deposits, the cheapness of labour, the successful introduction of iron for shipbuilding, the great advances in ship construction, and especially the wonderful progress of the steamship, had been able to give back to Great Britain her supremacy as a Mercantile Marine. And when the Civil War was over, America was too interested internally to pay a maximum amount of attention to ocean trading.

For the riches of the country were only beginning to be developed. Mines and manufactures, railroads and so on were now needing all the available capital. The New England shipyards, which for many years had been so valuable owing to the ample supplies of timber ready to hand, became unwanted in proportion as the Clyde, with its adjacent coalfields, was becoming more important for building ships of iron and then steel. It would be untrue to say that America ignored the building of iron ships, and in the early 'seventies she was interested in a mild way. The 'eighties passed without much enthusiasm for the subject, and then in 1894 and following year the Cramp shipyard launched the two fine transatlantic liners *St. Louis* and *St. Paul*, both being constructed of steel. There were many other steel ships built, and orders were received from abroad, but, broadly speaking, and in strict reference to merchant ships and not warships, America was not even now a shipbuilding country.

Those splendid schooners with which the port of Gloucester is forever associated, and those other sailing craft along the American coast do not alter the statement, nor do the vessels on the American lakes and rivers. We are thinking of ocean-going ships, which are the essential feature of any Mercantile Marine. The trade between the Atlantic and Pacific ports still remained for the old full-rigged clippers, because there were not enough cargoes east-bound to make it worthwhile for the steamship. And so America went on, content to allow her Merchant Service to be comparatively small and unprogressive.

But once again it required a war to call the national mind to consider what a Mercantile Marine means to a country. The Spanish war of 1898 did this to the extent that there was aroused a strong support for the Panama Canal project. The Act permitting this dates from 1892, and it is really from this year that the new phase begins, though only gradually. If you make direct and shorter roads on land leading to important trading centres, you obviously at once attract trade. If in the same manner you shorten communications by sea, it will have a similar effect. Quite apart from its warlike strategic value, which is outside our subject, the theory of the Panama Canal was based on the fact that it would reduce the sea route from New York to San Francisco by most of 8000 miles, and to Sydney and Yokohama by about 4000 miles. The 1892 Act also authorised admission to American registry of foreign-built vessels not more than five years old.

Then again came another war, the Great War, which began on August 4, 1914, the year in which the canal was opened. Too late America had begun to learn the value of a Mercantile Marine, and now she foresaw that there would be an inadequate supply of shipping to carry her trade across the ocean. Immediately she tried to make up for this by passing a law a fortnight after the outbreak of war removing the age limit in the Act of 1892. And now it becomes necessary to look into the matter somewhat closely, otherwise what followed is not intelligible.

When the European War broke out, America, having regard to her population, wealth, overseas trade and length of littoral, was in a curious position. The following figures are for June 1914, and are eloquent. In that month, of all the world's sea-going steel and iron steam tonnage the British Empire owned 47.7, Germany 12, Scandinavia 8.7, France 4.5, the United States 4.3 and Japan 3.9 *per cent*. As the war went on America realised at last that 71 *per cent*, of the world's steamships were in the hands of belligerents, and therefore the means of transport for American exports and imports—in other words, the exchange of wealth—had been taken away. Even farmers and cottongrowers who had never seen the sea in their lives began to take an interest in the subject when they suffered losses. It took the Great War to wake up the great American nation, as it had taken the American clippers to make our sailing ship-owners become active.

Shipbuilding in America suddenly began to revive, for from the end of 1915 ships were required by Britain, France and Norway. Mines and submarines had caused losses to the two first, while the third required more ships than ever for the profitable trade she was doing with Great Britain and France. Moreover, the American Mercantile Marine needed ships for herself; and the result was that in 1915 there was a net increase of nearly 500,000 tons added to its commercial service, including shipping which had been transferred to it. The position in the carrying trade outside America was this.

A large number of ships were interned in various ports, some thousands of tons had been sunk by the German mines and submarines, and yet the Allies were now requiring more for maintaining food for nations and supplies for the armies in the field. In addition to this, many ships had been taken from the Merchant Service for purely naval purposes and other objects, such as supply-vessels to the Fleet. And the unrestricted submarine campaign which Germany began in April 1917 was to make matters considerably worse; for in April of that year 545,282 tons of British merchant shipping alone were lost by enemy action.

It was on September 7, 1916, that Congress passed a law creating the United States Shipping Board, the original aim of which was to develop more effectively the American Mercantile Marine. A very few months later, on April 6, 1917, the United States declared war on Germany, and on May 4 the first American warships to reach Europe, consisting of six destroyers, steamed into Queens-town harbour. It is a day firmly fixed in my own memory, as the vessel I was then commanding was the first to go alongside them, north of Daunt's Rock lightship. Now with America a participant in the war, and about to send armies to Europe together with necessary military supplies, the need for American merchant tonnage became positively acute. In the whole of the United States there were not more than sixty- one shipyards, of which only thirty-seven were building steel craft.

But America realised that ships must be built at once, regardless of cost, both very quickly and in large numbers. Thus in a strange and romantic manner there came unexpectedly a revival of the wooden ship. An American writer has pointed out that of the entire transportation of American troops about 48¼ *per cent*, were carried in British ships, and 43 *per cent*, in American navy transports. But, with a fine patriotic effort, ship-building of all kinds now went ahead, and soon there were 341 shipyards building sea-going craft. Actually 1284 launching ways were now occupied. It was a remarkable lesson which war had taught in respect of the Mercantile Marine. There is no room to go into details, but it is sufficient to call attention to this exceptional effort, which showed what could be done. Fabricated ships, that is, vessels constructed by assembling the standardised plates made in the engineering shops, rendered possible only through the existence of numerous steel rolling mills, began to take the water; and if some of these craft were not always well built, we must remember that they were a temporary measure, and not intended to last.

The total construction of ships in the United States during the years 1910-1916 had averaged 450,000 tons a year. In 1917 it was nearly 1,000,000, in 1918 it was 3,223,506 tons, but in 1919 it was 6,558,823 tons, up to the end of the year in each case. These figures are given for the purpose of showing what can be done in a country which makes up its mind to have a commercial marine. America had been a long time learning its lesson, but there was no question that she had learned. Therefore it is not to be expected that she will let this hardly-acquired realisation be forgotten.

Indeed, the evidence is strongly the other way. On June 5, 1920, was approved the Merchant Marine Act for the promoting and maintaining an American Merchant Marine. It is sufficient evidence merely to read the declaration of policy as stated by Congress:

That it is necessary for the national defence and for the proper growth of its foreign and domestic commerce that the United States shall have a merchant marine of the best-equipped and most suitable types of vessels sufficient to carry the greater portion of its commerce and serve as a naval or military auxiliary in time of war or national emergency, ultimately to be owned and operated privately by citizens of the United States; and it is hereby declared to be the policy of the United States to do whatever may be necessary to develop and encourage the maintenance of such a merchant marine.

With the failure of any immediate benefits of this policy it is not necessary here to deal. But of all the many results of the Great War, few historically are more interesting than this revival. Competition between British and American shipping is inevitable, but it is merely a repetition of what happened in the clipper era; and we have seen that in the long run this spirit of emulation has always benefited the Merchant Service. Comparing the figures given above for June 1914, let us place alongside them those for June 1921, which are as instructive as the first. For now we find in the percentage of the world's total sea-going steel and iron steam tonnage that the British Empire owns 39.3, the United States 22.7, France and Japan each 5.6, but Scandinavia 7.7. Thus to have leapt from 4.3 to 22.7 in so short a space of time, and to have become second only to the British Empire, is a remarkable achievement.

The future remains to be seen. But we have noticed that the absence of competition caused the East Indian portion—and that was the greater part—of the British Mercantile Marine to get into a rut. It was only the opening-up to all of the East, the free and unfettered rivalry there and in the Atlantic, which brought about progress and improved conditions both for the trader and the passenger. In the face of the lessons of history, is it not better to welcome competition rather than to endeavour to hinder, by a series of laws which may do good, but may also cause international friction, more dreadful wars, and do little for the advancement of civilisation and the attainment of noble aims?

The practical value of history is that we are able to see at a glance the mistakes of our forefathers. If it is not that, it is a mere academic study. The world now realises that an adequate merchant fleet is as

necessary as an adequate fighting Navy. But it has required to be con-
fronted with big events before it could thoroughly grasp that essential
fact.

CHAPTER 19

The Minor Mercantile Marines

One important result of the war was to readjust the respective positions of the nations of the world in regard to their merchant fleets. Considering only steel and iron steam tonnage, the nations were in the following order of precedence immediately prior to the war: British Empire, Germany, Scandinavia, France, the United States', Japan, Holland, Italy, Austria-Hungary, Spain, Greece. But today the following is the order: British Empire, United States, and then there is an immense drop to Scandinavia, France, Japan, Italy, Holland, Spain, Germany and Greece about equal, and no Austro-Hungarian merchant ships. Whilst Scandinavia still occupies the third place, she represents only 7.7 of the world's steam tonnage as against the United States' 22.7 and the British Empire's 39.3.

Outside the belligerents the Scandinavians were the most important merchant fleet throughout the period of hostilities, and Norway was more important than Sweden. From the earliest times in European history the sea-spirit has been a real influence in Scandinavia, and some of the finest sailormen in the world have come from there. It is that spirit which has built up the Scandinavian merchant fleets, not merely through the sailing-ship days, but after. To them were sold many of Britain's clippers and other vessels as steam gradually became dominant; and even now they purchase obsolete British steamships, give them another name and put them into service again. The Allan liner *Virginian*, the first Atlantic turbine steamer, for instance, is now running in the Swedish-American Line.

The war found the Scandinavians with a comparatively large merchant fleet, not merely of steam vessels, but of sailing craft. Only those who were in the North Sea at that time could realise this fact, and as the years went on it became still more emphasised. For they were able to sell their agricultural produce to Germany for high prices, and they sold, also at a high rate, large supplies of food and of timber to Great Britain. The result was that the enormous demand for merchant ships brought great wealth to these North-men. They placed a large number of orders with British shipbuilding firms prior to peace, and in one area alone these orders amounted to 450,000 tons. But then came the slump, ships were not wanted, because trade became bad, many ship-owners were soon in financial straits and merchant captains found themselves without employment. The result is, that notwith-standing the boom, they owned in June 1921 only 7.7 as against 8.7 in June 1914 of the world's sea-going steam tonnage.

On the other hand, they have shown considerable enterprise in evolving the ocean-going motor ship. But whereas the Baltic meant so much to their shipping, the revolutionary upheavals in Russia and Germany have thoroughly disorganised that most important section of their trade. To take one instance alone, before the war, and even during those years, Sweden used to export in small steamships large quantities of iron ore to Germany, but now these exports have consid-erably diminished. Nevertheless, the possession of these Scandinavian merchant fleets, consisting as they do principally of small rather than big ships, is a strong factor to be considered in the future.

Today the French Mercantile Marine is of the same strength as Japan, owing to the last-mentioned country having gone ahead rather than the former having gone astern. The acquisition of a number of ex-German liners after the Armistice was something of a windfall, though it was a long time before some of the big craft were requisi-tioned. The Messageries Maritimes, for example, took over from the French Government the *Lucie Woermann* (4836 tons) and several big-ger ships. But as an influence in the shipping world, France is very dif-ferent from what she was during the time of Louis XIV and after. The naval architects and shipbuilders in France during the seventeenth and eighteenth centuries were in many cases as good, and frequently bet-ter than, those of England or Holland or Spain. But this supremacy had long since left them by the time the steamship became prevalent.

During the war the French Mercantile Marine was used entirely for the prosecution of the one great cause, but France lost during that period 1,129,000 out of 2,556,000 tons of merchant shipping with which she commenced hostilities. This has been more serious for France, because whilst during hostilities the shipyards of Great Britain, the United States and Japan were able to carry on building, the French yards were almost exclusively engaged in manufacturing for their armies. In fact, they were unable to launch more than 143,000 tons throughout the war, though afterwards about a hundred (ships were ordered in Great Britain, representing nearly 500,000 tons.

The French Mercantile Marine today consists of between 3,000,000 and 4,000,000 tons. Of this the fine big Atlantic liners running to New York make up a fair proportion, especially when we think of the 34,568-ton *Paris*, one of the largest liners afloat, and a singularly impressive ship to behold. As a result of the war Germany had to hand over to the Allies 521 ships, of nearly 3,000,000 tons displacement; and of these France was allotted 116, amounting to about 500,000 tons. But the greater part of her merchant fleet is based on the Mediterranean, running from Marseilles to the Black Sea, and her possessions in Asia and the Pacific, West Africa, and to North and South America. Most of her exports go to her colonies; and the short voyages across the Mediterranean to Algeria and Morocco, transporting corn, wine, sheep and vegetables, will ever be a valuable means of employing small tonnage ships. But it has needed a war to teach France that the whole of her ship-building and marine transportation required overhauling and revising.

Her shipping industry was based rather on the policy of making profits out of other industries than of becoming a means of creating new trade routes and fresh avenues to wealth. It is only now that she is realising the riches of her colonies which merely wait to be developed fully. To France, curiously enough, belonged the honour of owning the largest and finest sailing ship in the world. This was the *La France*. Fitted with auxiliary motors in the early days of the combustion engine, these were afterwards removed. She sailed out to the Pacific in 1922, but had the misfortune to pile up on a New Caledonian reef close to her destination and became a total wreck. Thus perished the last link France had with its former race of brilliant designers of sailing ships.

In the rise of nations few phenomena are more striking than the way the Japanese merchant fleet has leapt into prominence in so few years. Even before the war she possessed only 3.9 of the world's steam steel tonnage, and was the sixth power in the world as a sea-carrier; today she is actually bracketed fourth with France, and owning 5.6 of the percentage of tonnage. The Japanese are essentially copyists, and practically everything they know of shipbuilding or shipping in the modern sense has been derived from Great Britain.

The war came as a grand opportunity to them, and as soon as the Germans vanished from the Eastern trades, the Japanese stepped in and took what they wanted at a time when our traders were busy with other matters. Thanks to the heavy subsidies granted by their Government, they have put up a keen competition, including the Indian coasting trade. Both geographically and economically Japan is well situated so as to expand her merchant fleet throughout the Orient and the Pacific, and all the evidence points to her intention to take every advantage of her opportunities.

According to the most recent figures, the Japanese merchant fleet contained nearly 800 steamships of over 1000 tons, representing nearer 3,000,000 than 2,000,000 tons. The purchase of a large number of second-hand ships from other countries at a time when, owing to the slump, they could be bought for less than half their cost in Japan, is one of the latest instances of her enterprise. The Italian proportion of ownership in steamships has increased a point as a result of the war and after, and the addition in 1921 of the big *Giulio Cesare* was a considerable acquisition to such a small marine. Built in England, this 22,500-ton (gross) steamer was the largest vessel the Wallsend yard had launched since they constructed the *Mauretania*. She can do her nineteen knots and more, and being intended for the Genoa-Buenos Ayres route, was fitted with ample luxury to tempt the South Americans.

But there is also a big emigrant trade from this port westward, and more than half the accommodation in the ship is intended for them. The outcome of the war brought Trieste, Austria's only port, into the hands of Italy, and this may have an important effect on Italian shipping in the future. It used to be to Austria what Fiume was to Hungary, and both States used to give large subsidies to their Mercantile Marines and encourage transport to and from these ports. Just before the war the Austro-Hungarian merchant ships represented only slightly over one per cent, of all the world's sea-going steel steamers, but now this amount has dropped to nothing. Fiume was the port whence emigrants by the thousand poured from their Slav, Teuton and Magyar homes on board the liners bound for the United States. It was Hungary's only port, and then the World War put an end to its glory and made it a source of grave international anxiety.

But its close connection with the Mercantile Marine prosperity can be seen at once. For one steamship line alone used to take from there 30,000 emigrants annually. They used to run three steamships a month during the winters when bad harvests had caused the people to leave their homes for the New World, and each of these ships was carrying most of 2000. Then, having made $500 in America, they would for the most part return, and thus there was still further traffic for the shipping. The Austrian Lloyd Company owned about eighty steamships, though chiefly of small tonnage, but some were built in Trieste of about 4000 tons. With one steamship company the Hungarian Government actually entered into a contract, to last ten years, by which the former were to be guaranteed 30,000 emigrants a year; and a bonus of a hundred *francs* was to be paid for every passenger short of that number. It cannot be too much emphasised that the emigrant traffic has been one of the foundations of some steamship companies.

During the war the direct services from Scandinavia to America were strengthened; but the French emigrant traffic has never been great. Before the war the Italian steamship lines were largely under German influence. No emigrants could be carried to or from Italy except in a licensed ship; and a vessel more than three years old, not previously employed in the Italian service, could not receive a licence unless her speed was at least eighteen knots. But from the European continent by far the greatest emigrant traffic went from Bremen and Rotterdam in the two big German lines.

The present position of Holland and Spain, almost at the bottom of the list, shows pathetically that a country which in its day has been the greatest sea-carrier, which owned and built the finest ships in the world, may in a century or more be pushed out of the struggle unless her fighting fleet is able to secure free passage for the merchant vessels. Holland, at least, owns a small fleet of first-class liners, principally for the North American trade and to the Dutch East Indies. With regard to the former, Rotterdam has been to them a useful port for attracting a good many emigrants every year. Prior to the war the German lines were too wise to compete against the Dutch, preferring not to separate forces in concentrating against the Cunard and White Star Lines. Most Dutch steamship hues enjoy a measure of support from the Dutch railways, but in the past there was also a good deal of support from Germany.

The future of Mercantile Marines is the future of trade itself; for shipping not merely takes goods to market, but actually creates those markets in localities hitherto undeveloped. The sailing ship as an ocean-carrier is certainly fast disappearing, and everything now is reckoned on a basis of economy, but with strict regard to speed and efficiency. The need for shipping, apart from temporary slumps in the cycle of trade through prosperity to depression, must increase as the resources of the world become greater. If the tramp steamer forces her way up a shallow river and finds an abundance of a certain commodity which by some sudden turn in social life is much in demand in London or New York, this new trade will go on and on until a town is built on the banks, the river is dredged, and eventually liners call there not for cargoes, but to bring passengers.

The town needs its regular mail service, the inhabitants require costly manufactured goods from England or America; and so, in the end, it grows to be a colony with its own special exports and imports. The arrival of every ship increases the trade, agents from commercial corporations land and start a new vein of development. Finally, after a couple of centuries, perhaps, the colony decides to have its own merchant fleet, and after it has got thoroughly used to this, and had some risk of war, it realises that its Merchant Marine must be protected by a fighting navy. Today Australia has its own liners, and navy, and yet it was only in 1788 that the first thousand settlers landed there. In the exchange of wealth the sea is, so to speak, the counter across which the deal is done. You may live inland and forget all about the sea; you may hate it or you may fear it; but it is there all the time, and it means everything to any ambitious community. It is by means of the merchant ship that the sea is, partially at least, controlled for the sake of land development and the convenience of communities.

A FAST DISAPPEARING SHIP

CHAPTER 20

The Future of the Mercantile Marine

If the attention of the reader has been thus far secured, he will have appreciated the fact that to any nation owning a seaboard the possession of a Mercantile Marine is as important as having a fighting navy. We have seen that Great Britain, the United States, France, Germany, Japan—not to mention the rest—all realise more than ever the prime importance of an efficient and adequate merchant fleet. You find this in the official statements as well as in the remarks by their shipping experts. As we said at the beginning of this volume, it has taken a great war to cause this right thinking, but you may be assured that from now onwards the merchant fleets are coming into their own, and the service is going to be regarded before long with some of the old respect that was ascribed to it in the palmiest days of the sailing ship.

It is sea-borne trade which makes a Mercantile Marine. It is the great coalfields conveniently near big harbours that have helped to build up the modem British marine after her shipping was temporarily eclipsed by the American. The development of the world consequent on the coming of the industrial age, the great increase of overseas trade therefrom resulting, caused a loud and universal call for cheap maritime carriage. The steamer satisfied that call, for the reason that she was built economically near to the coalfields, and economically propelled because she had cheap coal. She could therefore afford to carry goods cheaply. Then, as we have also seen, this tramp is the forerunner of the liner, and so the story goes on like a stone gathering momentum as it comes down the mountain.

So it all depends on cheap fuel quite as much as on cheap labour. The Scandinavians have had the latter for years, but it never enabled them to build up such a merchant fleet as one might have expected. The world's greatest shipping centre today is the Port of London, notwithstanding the great set-back it received during the war, when the presence of German submarines in the English Channel diverted much of its ancient trade to western ports. Had it not been for the possession of an enormous merchant fleet, consisting of a large proportion of small and moderate-sized steamers, the Allied cause would most certainly have been lost, irrespective of the army in the field or the navy at sea. The British and German blockades, though exerted in the one case by big ships and in the latter by submarines, had the same effect: the paralysing of the merchant fleet. Take the blockade away and the war could have gone on as long as a couple of men were alive. The pivot of the whole thing is therefore the merchant ship, and she in turn depends on her fuel.

The fuel of the future will be oil, and you will find only a minority of experts to deny this. Whether aircraft will ever become the principal passenger-carriers over the world is possible, but remote. For the carriage of goods the dependence will remain on merchant shipping, and one of the incentives to the use of oil-fuel will be brought about by increased competition. Oil is the more economical fuel, for the reason that, other things being equal, one ton of oil-fuel as now used in Diesel engines drives a vessel three times as far as one ton of coal burnt under the boilers of a steamship. And yet oil is twice as efficient as coal when the ship has water-tube boilers and geared turbines. This is the statement of Sir Westcott Abell, the Chief Ship Surveyor of Lloyd's Register. The biggest liners have now been converted into oil-burning, and it is conceivable that before long we may have Diesel-engined Atlantic leviathans instead of steamers. The absence of boilers will mean more room for passengers and cargo, therefore increased earning capacity.

Whether we think of oil as used for Diesel or for steam engines, it certainly looks as if the future Mercantile Marines of the world will be in the main oil-driven. In that case the outlook for the British Mercantile Marine, which has been based on cheap coal, may cause some anxiety. The possession of ample oilwells in other parts of the world may, and probably will, get over the difficulty; but it is one thing to have coalfields at home, and quite another consideration to fetch oil from the other end of the earth.

Moreover the commercial fight for oil-areas may conceivably lead to international strife, and the prolongation of the war might depend on how long the supplies of oil could be maintained for the shipping. In any forecast of the world's Mercantile Marines due regard must therefore be paid to the use and supply of oil.

The introduction of oil-fuel into the modern Atlantic ships has done away with the old, laborious work of stoking, and necessitated from the fireman a higher skill, more technical knowledge and keener concentration; and he has to be on the move continually in order to see that the burners are in good order and the flame is continuous. During bad weather, or fogs, fires can be extinguished, and thus economy gained. More bunker-fuel is being consumed on the ocean at the present than ever, and although during the last twenty years a complete revolution has been made in the engine-room by the use of turbines and geared turbines, it is only with the introduction of oil-fuel that the stokehold has become more progressive. In many cases ex-naval men are now employed in the British oil-fuel liners. Their experience of years in oil-fuel ships well fits them for this skilled "stoking" in the modern merchant-men. And here may be the beginning of another improvement.

It is well known that the crew's accommodation in most men-of-war is superior to that in most merchantmen, especially in regard to cleanliness. During the war it was surprising to naval officers commanding armed merchant cruisers that such conditions were allowed in liners which would never be tolerated in fighting ships. One British admiral, in particular, was so impressed as to express his opinions afterwards in print. Now, if the introduction of highly skilled ratings from the navy continues, it may be taken as certain that the standard of life in the crew's quarters will become higher and thus a high-grade type of man will be attracted. There is going to be a general levelling up in the Mercantile Marines of the world, so long as there is peace assured. The world is wearied of war, and asks only to be allowed to develop its resources in peace. Everyone nowadays is interested in commerce, and the time will come when the practice which existed in the East India Company's ships will be reverted to.

Only the sons of the best families will be thought to be good enough for the national merchant ships: only the best sons will offer themselves for the honour of controlling the ships which maintain the country's life-giving trade. In the time of the Elizabethans, before the East India Company; in the Spanish and Portuguese and Venetian trade supremacies, the pick of the nation were engaged in overseas commerce; and in the twentieth century, when so much technical knowledge, so much responsible capability are required of a man, none but the best types of officers and men should be accepted or offered.

Permanent employment, good pay, pride in ship and service, high standard of accommodation, and the most careful selection of candidates will go a long way towards bringing about this desired end.

In the olden days the sailor was a very gallant fellow, whose job it was to go aloft and lay out along a yard and handsail in the foulest weather. At sea he was heroic; on shore he was often a drunken reprobate. Things have altered. The modern shipman is just as gallant, as we know from his exploits afloat during the war. But he is better educated, uses his head more and his fists less. He reads and thinks and reasons for himself, and if he knows nothing of the old seafaring, he is highly skilled in the working of the hundreds of wonderful appliances which are essential to the modern merchant ship. To him the shore is not always symbolical of debauch. He is better treated than his ancestors, and his undoubted rights have begun to be respected. The result is that there is a general improvement going on through the Mercantile Marine not merely in regard to the ships themselves, but in the personnel.

The romance of the sailing-ship days has to be merged today in the bigger romance of sea-borne trade. It is ridiculous to say, as one lecturer recently stated, that the Mercantile Marine has no fine traditions like the navy, and therefore there is no enthusing force at the back of it. To make such a statement—and I regret to say that it was uttered by a distinguished merchant ship captain—is to be ignorant of sea history. During the recent war, during all the previous wars, through the ages of peace, back and back as far as we have any records, you will find the marine merchantman doing fine things, piling up the finest traditions. If that is not so, the whole purpose of this volume has been missed. I have endeavoured to show what the Mercantile Marine has done for the world throughout time in all kinds of ships. Sailors are a conservative race, and there is at heart very little difference between the best of each century. To them we all owe more than we can ever repay or even realise.

Whether the average merchant ship of the future is to be the cruiser-stern vessel with oil-fuel and geared turbines, or with Diesel engines, matters less than the spirit which animates the officers and men. In the British Mercantile Marine the officers are drawn from many sources, but the chief training establishments are in the *Worcester*, lying in the Thames, the *Conway*, lying in the Mersey, and in the Nautical College, Pangbourne. It is to these three institutions especially that we look for the future mercantile officer, on whom great responsibilities rest for the upholding and carrying on of the magnificent heritage of tradition. In the United States this preparation for the sea is being carried out with that thoroughness which was shown during the war for making sailors out of raw landsmen. The recruiting for the American Mercantile Marine, according to the latest official report to hand, already consisted of a personnel which was 68 per cent. American.

Its Sea Training Bureau has training stations and training ships, and in the first three years turned out between 80,000 and 40,000 unlicensed ratings. In addition, there are the Navigation and Engineering Schools and advanced courses for men already holding licences. Such subjects as the operation, repair, adjustment and general upkeep of marine turbines, and matters dealing with electricity and oil, are included in the last-mentioned *curricula*. The result was that in four years licences were granted to over 10,000 graduates as masters, first, second and third mates, chief engineers, first, second and third assistant engineers.

And by means of a Sea Service Bureau maintained at various Atlantic, Gulf and Pacific coast ports, during one year over 100,000 officers and men were placed in United States ships. Thus, with glorious traditions behind them, and an equally glorious future in front, the Mercantile Marines of the nations of the maritime world have every reason to be proud of their respective services. Competition there assuredly will be, not merely between British and American, but, presently, German merchant fleets.

That is all for the good of the services concerned and for the world in general. The lesson from past history is that maritime legislation in the long run is better omitted except where it is necessary as a reply to that of another country setting up unfair competition. The real freedom of the seas is to allow the merchant ship to pursue her way freely, unhampered; and to find her trade where she can, and be allowed to develop that trade as it has been in the past by Venetian, Spaniard, Dutch, Briton, American and others. To interfere with this system is to court trouble which in the long run fails to benefit the very organisation it was intended to protect.

Navigation laws are all very well in intention; but far better still is it to allow free trading over the seas, free flow of emigrants and commerce, fair opportunities for all. The best must win in the last instance, but why not let each marine go about its own business as each trading concern ashore is allowed to carry on its own affairs? The merchant fleets mean too much to be controlled by the State in any country, except under exceptional circumstances and with the most weighty excuse. That is one of the lessons in the history of our subject, and we may leave it at that.

Appendix

SAILS OF THE ESSEX EAST INDIAMAN

The following is a list of the sails which the Essex could set, and it is worth placing on record now that the sailing ship is so rapidly becoming a rarity. These details have been taken from a contemporary manuscript which has been kindly sent me by Colonel E. B. Urmston, C.B., whose great-grandfather served in East Indiamen from the time when he joined as a midshipman in 1763, and afterwards commanded several of these ships between 1783 and 1803.

In 1795 he brought home, as Commodore, a fleet of thirty East Indiamen without a convoy of any of H.M. ships, and later in the same year was Commodore of the East Indiamen fleet which accompanied Sir Ralph Abercrombie's expedition to the West Indies. His eldest son, Sir James Urmston, joined the company's service as a "writer" in 1798, and became President of the company's factory and affairs in China.

This memorandum, already turning yellow with age, was made in 1816, at the time Lady Urmston came home in the *Essex*, and with the aid of existing pictures of East Indiamen it would not be impossible to reconstruct a model on fairly accurate lines. It will be seen that she was able to set twenty-seven sails on her foremast, twenty-one on her mainmast, and seventeen on her mizzen: total sixty-five. It is interesting as showing that at least one of these Indiamen was a real sail-carrier. She was commanded by Captain Nisbett.

Fore course
,, topsail
,, t'gallant sail
,, royal
,, skysail
,, moon-raker
,, cloud-scraper
,, star-gazer
,, storm staysail
,, topmast staysail
Jib
Inner jib
Flying ,,
Outer ,,
Cutter's topmast jib
Upper ,,

On the bowsprit:
Sprit sail
Sprit topsail
,, outer topsail

Studding sails:
Common lower studding sail
Outer lower studding sail
Common topmast studding sail
Outer topmast studding sail
Common t'gallant studding sail
Outer t'gallant studding sail
Royal t'gallant studding sail

Main course
,, topsail
,, t'gallant sail
,, royal
,, skysail
,, moon-raker
,, cloud-scraper
,, star-gazer
,, staysail
,, topmast staysail
,, middle ,,
,, t'gallant ,,
,, royal ,,
,, upper ,,

Lower studding sail
Common topmast studding sail
Outer topmast studding sail
Common t'gallant studding sail
Outer t'gallant studding sail
Royal t'gallant studding sail
Upper t'gallant studding sail

Square cross jackyard
Mizzen topsail
,, t'gallant sail
,, royal
,, skysail
,, moon-raker

Driver
Ring-tail
Watersail
Gaff topsail
Upper ,,
Mizzen staysail
,, topmast staysail
,, t'gallant ,,

Mizzen royal staysail
,, topmast stuns'l
,, t'gallants'l